Stories of Crime in Liverpool by ex-Detective Sergeant William Prendergast.

Also in Arrow Books by William Prendergast

Calling All Z-Cars

William Prendergast

Crime Scene

ARROW BOOKS

ARROW BOOKS LTD
178–202 Great Portland Street, London W1

AN IMPRINT OF THE HUTCHINSON GROUP

London Melbourne Sydney
Auckland Bombay Toronto
Johannesburg New York

*

First published as *Z-Car Squad*
by John Long Limited 1968
Arrow edition 1969

Made and printed in Great Britain
by The Anchor Press Ltd,
Tiptree, Essex

09 002452 4

For John, Frank and Nell

Contents

Author's Foreword

When I retired after thirty-two years in the Liverpool C.I.D. I had no plans to become a writer. True, my mind was crammed with stories, but I had no notion of what to do with them.

Then the B.B.C. decided to mount a television series about the working lives of uniformed and plainclothes police officers. It is now a matter of history that *Z-Cars* changed the entire fictional approach to a subject which has intrigued writers ever since Edgar Allan Poe invented the detective story.

For the first time millions of people were seeing a television series stamped with the astringent seal of authenticity and a kind of laconic yet compassionate realism. I was invited to make my case-book material available to the writers of the series and later I became police consultant to the programme.

Z-Cars—which evolved from a four-part comedy series called *Jacks and Knaves* and a TV play entitled *Who, Me?*—uses this case-book material as a basis for its fictional stories. They are, by all odds, a brilliant evocation of police work in fictionalised documentary form.

The success of the programme brought a request for me to write my real-life detective stories in book form, and *Z-Car Detective* was the result. I had become a writer—something I had never envisaged. And this was not the end. So many people liked the book that my publishers called for a second autobiographical volume, which appeared last year under the title of *Calling All Z-Cars*.

Both books were so popular that a request came through for a third. I have called it *Crime Scene*. In this I have again sought to illuminate the attitudes and inner drives not only of the police but of the tearaways themselves, for always I have tried to cut below the surface and find out what happens deep inside the human façade.

As in my previous volumes, I am telling most of the stories in the first person. Where it is necessary to depart temporarily from the limitations of this literary device by reporting conversations and narration which occurred when I was not actually present, the reconstruction is based on acute questioning and detailed research.

But the facts in my stories are the true stuff of reality—tragedy and comedy, goodness and viciousness, fears and fulfilment; often inextricably mixed-up together, as indeed they are in life everywhere. Only the names have been changed.

I hope you will like reading them . . . and perhaps put the book down with a deeper insight into the minds and hearts of the men and women who people its pages.

W.P.

1

The Wrong Jack

It was 11.15 on the hottest night of the summer and the atmosphere in the big detectives' room at Liverpool City Police Headquarters was as heavy as a waterlogged boat.

Tired men with incipient cigarette coughs and sweat lakes spreading darkly across the backs of crumpled shirts sat at desks waiting for midnight. This is the hour when the duty rota changes—the time policemen call the witching hour, the hiatus created by one mob going off duty and another moving in. The tearaways know about it, too; for them it is the best of all times to do a job.

I was pondering this occupational hazard instead of finishing a routine report on an ill-used typewriter when Alderson, the desk sergeant, thrust his grey head round the door and said: 'Z Victor One reports a break-in at Conn's jewellery store in Franklin Street.'

My eyes went automatically to the big wall-clock. The hands were jerking to 11.21. 'Hell,' I said.

Alderson grinned. 'It's all right, you don't need to go out, Bill,' he said amiably. 'Johnny's with the Z-car squad.'

I picked my jacket off the chair back and struggled into it. Sweat pressed coldly against my spine. 'I'd better go, just the same,' I growled.

'You're due off at midnight and Johnny Dallas is already on the scene, but you can't resist a case,' said

Alderson. 'I believe you'd cut short a holiday on the Isle of Capri at the prospect of an investigation.'

'Capri?' I echoed. 'Where would a working Jack get the money to take a holiday there?'

'You're sort of a prudent man, you must have tons of it salted away,' said Alderson, making a very straight face.

'If I took those kind off holidays I wouldn't have anything for my old age.'

'You can live on the pension when the time comes, you don't need so much when you're knocking on.'

'That's a fallacy invented by fellas with plenty in the bank.'

'Well, anyway, the missus'll be expecting you home about a quarter after midnight. Unless, of course she's given up ever expecting to have you home on time.'

I thought the latter more than probable, and reflected, not for the first time, that a lot of a police detective's wife is less than easy. I knew well enough that I didn't really need to go out on this break-in. Detective Constable Johnny Dallas was there now with Bert Rawlings and Jock Ewing. A good, ambitious young Jack with a good uniformed team. I didn't have to go there, but I knew I was going.

'I've got my own car, I can look in on the way home,' I said.

'That's just compromising,' said Alderson. 'You go straight home.'

'I'll just stop for a few minutes,' I called over my shoulder.

I was going through the main office when Alderson leaned across the counter and said: 'I'll ring your home and tell the wife you'll be a bit late, shall I?'

'All right.'

'Not,' said Alderson, 'that it'll be news to Alice, I'm thinking.'

It was cooler outside, but not much, and when I got my car out of the police parking yard it was like opening the door of an oven in a waterfront café short of air space. I wound both windows down and drove north along Lime Street. It was emptied alike of traffic and stray pedestrians. I went past the Empire Theatre and made a short series of turns into Franklin Street. Lights were blazing in Conn's store, but there was no sign of Z Victor One.

I tramped across the pavement. The door of the shop opened and a small young fellow peered short-sightedly at me. He was no more than five feet five tall and about twenty-three years old. He was wearing a shiny blue serge suit and a white shirt without a tie and his eyes blinked agitatedly. He was a hunchback.

'Police,' I said. 'Prendergast, detective sergeant, C.I.D.'

The nervous expression faded. He held the door wide open. I went through, following him as he moved with short, awkward steps.

'I'm Benny Foy,' he offered. 'I work here.'

I put what must have been the twenty-ninth cigarette of the day in my mouth, had second thoughts and returned it to the packet. My throat was already as parched as the Sahara Desert.

'Where's the Z-car crew?'

'They've gone. The detective who was with them got a clue.'

'He did?'

'Yeh, that's right. A very nice fella. Detective Constable Dallas. He thought he knew the way to—er—apprehend the miscreants who broke in here.'

'I see. Where's the boss?'

'He's sick. The flu. It's bad when you get the flu in

this hot weather. I mean it's worse than in the cold, if you know what I mean, Mr. Prendergast.'

I said I knew what he meant and added: 'I take it you've told Mr. Conn?'

'I phoned, just after I called the police. The Z-car fellas came very quickly, I was surprised how quick they came.'

'Their route was in your neighbourhood, Mr. Foy. But you were telling me about Detective Dallas finding a clue?'

'That's right, I was. A small bit of paper or card it was. He found it behind the safe, in the office. He seemed to think it'd help.'

'I see,' I said again, though I wasn't seeing very much. 'What did the gang get away with?'

'Two hundred and seventy-nine pounds was in the safe. We had a good day. It's all gone.'

'A lot, isn't it, to leave in the safe?'

'That's what I told Mr. Conn, but he thought it'd be all right till morning and he didn't really want to be bothered owing to having the flu.'

A thought came to me and I said: 'How did you happen to be here after hours, Mr. Foy?'

'I live here, above the shop,' the little hunchback explained simply. 'Mr. Conn he gave me a job as his assistant and he lets me have the room above. He is very kind to me, especially because . . .' He let the sentence stay unfinished.

'Because perhaps you find it a little hard to get work?'

'Yes. People are sort of put off like because I'm deformed. Some of them think I'm what I'm not.'

'Vicious or something?'

'Yes, sir.' His underlip trembled fractionally. Then he went on in a composed voice: 'I'm not like that, Mr. Prendergast.'

I looked at his misshapen body, at his slightly twisted

face, and wondered at the senseless injustices of life. 'I don't think that, Benny,' I said quietly.

'Thanks, boss.' He smiled. 'Johnny Dallas doesn't think so, either. I hope he gets those villains.'

'Johnny's a good Jack, so happen he will,' I said. 'Do you mind if I look around while I'm here?'

He made a gesture with one of his short, thick arms. I went into the office. I didn't find anything. If there had been a clue Johnny had picked it up. I went out to my car and drove back to Headquarters. Alderson was gone. George Bull, the late-duty sergeant, was behind the long counter.

'Thought you'd gone home, P,' he offered. 'Though I did hear that . . .' He broke off as a scuffle sounded beyond the main entrance doors.

Johnny Dallas came through them with Rawlings and Ewing. They flanked a couple of tearaways. I knew them all right—Tim Goulden and Big Mick Flannery.

'I want to see me lawyer,' Big Mick bellowed.

'Och, you'll no see any lawyer until you've seen the inside of the cells,' snorted Jock Ewing. His left eye was purpling.

'Where'd you get the shiner?' asked Bull interestedly.

'From this fella.' Jock glared at Big Mick.

What's the charge?' I asked.

'Breaking and entering and stealing two hundred and seventy-nine pounds, property of Julius Conn,' answered Dallas.

'How'd you get them Johnny?'

'One of these villains accidentally dropped a torn bit of a club membership card and I spotted it. Membership of the Three Jacks Club—an apt title, as you might say. An all-night boozing club. We went there and caught these fellas in a back room counting the loot.'

'Nice work.'

'Well, I had the luck.'

'You spotted that small bit of pasteboard. You could have overlooked it.'

'Then I'd have been a poor detective.'

'I want to see me lawyer, I tell yer,' shouted Flannery.

'You haven't even got one, I'll bet,' said Rawlings.

'I'll get one, see.'

Bull looked disgustedly at him. 'Take them away and book them,' he said. 'They can get a lawyer when they've been put down.'

Johnny lit a cigarette. He looked pleased without being cocky about it. He was only twenty-four and had been promoted to C.I.D. less than a year previously. By my book he was about the best recruit the department had taken in for a long time. I had liked him from the start. He had been a good cop on the beat when he joined the force as a green young constable from somewhere up on the Fylde coast, just as I had done many years before. I knew he was ambitious and that he had the educational background which would help him to pass examinations. He also had an engaging personality, which made him the easiest of colleagues to get along with. Johnny worked hard. He also played hard—perhaps, at times, a little too hard. But he was young and the young are entitled to have a good time.

'Big Mick won't talk,' I said.

'No, I shouldn't think so. I'll formally charge them and then get a statement from Benny Foy. Anyway, we caught them red-handed. I'll go along and see Benny shortly. After that—sleep.' He yawned widely, though no man ever looked less tired.

'I'll tell you one thing, Johnny,' I mused.

'What's that?'

'You've made a friend for life out of Benny Foy.'

'He's a nice little fella. I like him.'

'He worships you. I could tell. It was in his face.'

'Hell, I'm just a Jack doing a job,' grinned Johnny.

II

Seven months went by. Big Mick Flannery and Tim Goulden were behind the grim walls of Walton Jail, not that this was a new experience for either of them. Cases came and some were solved and some weren't, because you can't win all the time.

I saw Benny Foy once or twice around this period. I knew that he had struck up a close friendship with Johnny Dallas—a curious friendship in some ways because Johnny liked to spend his free time enjoying himself, which meant girls and dances and theatre-going.

One night when we were driving together he said: 'You were right about making a lifelong friend out of Benny. He's not really my sort, if you know what I mean, but he's a great little fella. Barmy about police work and thinks I'm a sort of all-purpose Sherlock Holmes and Chief Superintendent of Scotland Yard all rolled into one. Police business fascinates him. If he hadn't been born a hunchback he'd probably have made a good copper himself.'

'Happen he would.'

'It's funny, though, the way he seems to have taken to me.'

'It's not, you know. You treated him as a normal human being the first time you met.'

Johnny flushed slightly. 'Hell, why not?' he demanded. 'Benny's a good kid. Anyone can see that.'

'A lot don't, from what he told me,' I said.

A month later Johnny was married. He met a beautiful Irish-Welsh girl at the dance and they more or less swept each other off their feet. I went to the wedding and

I never saw two people look happier than Johnny Dallas and Maureen Jones.

Sam Goodyard, the D.I. at Headquarters, was drinking a pint with me that night when he said, without any preamble: 'There's a bit of a shake-up coming along, Bill. I'm going.'

'What d'you mean, you're going? Going where?'

'Divisional H.Q.' Goodyard eyed me levelly and went on: 'Frank Arnold will be taking my place.'

I didn't answer immediately. Arnold had been with us as a detective sergeant. Then he was switched to a regional force down South. I had heard that he was doing well there. He was a big, floridly handsome man in his middle forties with a face full of teeth and virility, ambitious and socially aspiring. I neither liked nor disliked him, but I wasn't giving three cheers at the news that he was taking over from Sam Goodyard.

'You don't think much of it, Bill, do you?' asked the D.I. quietly.

'Not a lot, no.'

'Is that all you've got to say?'

'It's enough. I'm going to have to work with him.'

'You'll do that all right.' Goodyard ordered two more pints. 'He'll not mess you about.'

I turned this over in my mind. Then I said: 'You mean he's the type who'll surround himself with men who fit into his particular pattern or can be induced to, and I'm not likely to be one of them?'

'Yes, that's about it.' Goodyard looked vaguely troubled. 'I dare say I shouldn't be talking to you this way, but we're friends as well as colleagues and I thought you ought to know how things stand. It's been a ... well, a sort of political intrigue behind the scenes. Some of the higher-ups fancy Arnold and they carried enough weight to get him the post when the opportunity arose.'

'Or was made to happen?'

Goodyard's lean mouth twitched faintly. 'You don't miss anything, I'll say that for you.' he answered. 'Well all right then, some of the top brass have been playing a little private power game and Frank Arnold is the man they wanted. Mind you, it's not bad for me. Just a transfer and good prospects with it. All the same . . .'

He hesitated and seemed about to drop the subject, but I was in no mood to let him. 'All the same, you're worried about something, Sam,' I prompted.

'A little, yes.'

'Do you want to tell me or not?'

'I wasn't going to, but I believe I will. I'm worried about the kind of influence Arnold is likely to exercise on the younger fellows,' Goodyard said. 'There's Carter, Ackroyd and, perhaps not least, Dallas. All eager young chaps anxious not to put the wrong foot forward.'

'You said *perhaps not least* about Johnny Dallas—why?'

'You don't need to ask that, Bill,' the D.I. said.

'You mean I know Johnny is a good personality man, that he's recently married and anxious to get ahead fast?'

Sam Goodyard nodded.

'But that's not all you mean, is it, Sam?'

He answered indirectly. 'What's your rating of his character?'

'I like him.'

'I didn't ask you that.'

'All right then. I think Johnny has the makings of a brilliant policeman. I think he has brains, education, willingness to work and the flair to go with it.'

'Virtues, Bill, virtues. What about weaknesses?'

'Only one, I think. He's always liked a good time. He still likes it, even though he's married. I don't mean he chases skirts, I don't believe that for a single moment.

But he likes living well. Too much of that becomes a weakness.'

Goodyard peered into his tankard as if half expecting to surprise guilty secrets. When he raised his eyes to mine he said: 'Correct. That means he's exactly the sort of up-and-coming young Jack that Frank Arnold will go after.'

'Well?'

'Oh, give over, you know what I mean. Arnold is an efficient officer, but he's the kind—thank God we don't get them too often—who can reduce a talented youngster to the status of a fetcher and carrier and general mouthpiece. You've seen it happen and I've seen it. Every cop knows it goes on. Like I say, not often, but it can and does happen.'

'Policemen are people, too,' I said. 'I can see the danger all right. Perhaps if I chatted Johnny up a bit?'

'Yes, he might take it from you,' Goodyard reflected. 'He likes you personally.'

'I'll see what I can do, then. When do you leave?'

'Within the next fortnight. Arnold will be here at weekend to look us over.'

'What does the Chief Constable think about it?'

'I'll have to chat *him* up a bit,' said the D.I. with a grin.

Well, I had no trouble with Frank Arnold. For some years now I had been allowed a fairly wide area of freedom, in the sense that I could work at cases without detailed briefing from the top. I am, I suppose, a somewhat fiercely independent man; some have even called me difficult. I think what they mean is that I don't take over-direction very well. But no one in the service has ever charged me with lack of application to duty. In fact, I have always been prone to give up much of my private time to the work—provided I could go at it in my own way. There had grown up a sort of unofficial recognition that, within reasonable limits, I could handle investigations without slavish observance of the book. It had worked more than well enough, and Detective Inspector Frank Arnold made no attempt to change the set-up as far as I was concerned.

But I would have had to be half blind not to observe changes—slow at first, then rapidly accelerating—which were taking place under his command. Specifically in relation to Detective Johnny Dallas. Inside weeks of the onset of the power shake-up Johnny was a drinking companion of the new boss of the C.I.D. room. Within months he was switched to the 'easy pickings' of the waterfront beat. Exactly as Sam Goodyard had predicted, Johnny Dallas became a mouthpiece and fetcher and carrier for Frank Arnold.

Along the vast line of the docks there were many pubs where the licensee was more than happy to cultivate the friendship of a C.I.D. man. It gave them a certain feeling of safety to have a detective on their side—safety both during the day when the Dock Road zone swarmed with rough and tough men, and at night when danger might stalk the seemingly deserted streets. It was reassuring when a friendly Jack wandered in for a drink. Often plainclothes men working the dock beat struck up firm friendships with ships' pursers, chief stewards, storekeepers and the like—and it was good for trade when a Jack brought his pals into a favourite pub for a drink. Nor was this all. If Jack was so minded, there was always something he could get from the crews—meals and drinks and other 'perks'—so that crime was not the sole purpose of the daily visits to the ships in dock.

The dock detail was a necessary assignment, but it was a potentially soul-destroying one to an ambitious detective or uniformed man. And to any man with a fondness for the fleshpots the temptations were too easy and too plentiful. Arnold knew all this well enough—and it suited his purpose. He wanted a fetcher and carrier he could trust when he himself wanted some of the pickings, so Johnny Dallas was his instant choice. Arnold had percieved a small weakness in Johnny's make-up as surely as Sam Goodyard and myself.

The waterfront beat had yet another slant. It was useful for the Jack to have a 'drop' where he could pick up his stuff to take home after he had finished his tour. Sometimes he brought grub along for the licensee as well as for the home stakes. And if there was 'trouble' at home the Jack could always stay with his 'friend', feeding with the family at the pub—and such an association began for Johnny at The Mainbrace.

His young wife was the daughter of a bank manager who was, well, not over-enthusiastic about his son-in-law being a cop. Even after marrying Johnny and with a baby on the way, Maureen Dallas was still very much under the influence of her parents; so much so that she spent more time with them than in her new home. Often Johnny had to call for her there because she did not like being left on her own in the house Johnny had provided. Nor did she care to mix with the wives of other policemen. Many times she stayed for days on end with her parents, saying it would be better for the child to come. All that kind of thing. You could almost see the marriage falling apart. I am not saying this to condone Johnny's conduct—a man should find the strength to survive both the triumphs and the disillusion of life—but it was a contributing factor.

Unfortunately, Johnny was unable to find this inner strength. He teamed-up first with an old hand in the C.I.D. whose only idea was to get as much booze down during duty hours as was compatible with getting through his tour along the waterfront. Then Johnny himself was moved to the dock beat and soon he was using supposed long hours of duty as an excuse for his failure to go home promptly. When his baby daughter was born it was his parents-in-law who made all the arrangements; Johnny was scarcely consulted. The joy which he should have known as a young father was soured by the growing rift between himself and his wife—the increasing rows, the unanswered pleas for her to spend more time with him in the home he had made. To an unhappy, increasingly embittered man with a weakness for a so-called 'good time' the transfer to the dock beat was not less than a disaster.

But, what the hell, he was getting well in with his boss, wasn't he? Oh, yes—too well. Yet only a handful of years previously Arnold, believing he had been passed over for promotion, nearly resigned. Then, in the sudden power rise which can erupt in the police service just as easily as in big business, the old gang moved out and the new lot taking over, Frank Arnold got a new and better lease of professional life.

When this happens the first move is to set up your yes-men, gathering a team of subordinates who will strengthen your power. And more than any other man, Johnny Dallas was 'in' . . . though exactly what he was in for he did not yet know.

Soon he was more welcome at The Mainbrace pub than at his own home. He could run up a bill or tap for a few quid if he lost on the horses. And he was now a favourite among the ships' officers whose excessive hospitality tied him to them. Nothing illegal—a couple of bottles of Scotch, extra grub, little presents, cigarettes for good old Johnny and his mates. Johnny Dallas was being shown around all right. Now he was a *bon vivant*, a good fella—do a good turn for anybody.

Frank Arnold knew this was almost certain to happen because he already knew all about Johnny's disintegrating marital life, his boozing and gambling. But it suited him to have Johnny on the dock beat. What did it matter if a man's whole personality was being sapped? He could always find another if Johnny finally got out of line. There are always second-raters eager to catch the crumbs that fall from the boss's executive table. 'Damned sad about young Dallas—I gave him every chance. but he threw them away. Too bad.'

More than once I tried to pull Johnny out of the mess he had drifted into. I ought to have known better, because this kind of advice is rarely accepted and never welcomed.

'I'm doing fine, Bill,' Johnny said. 'What the hell are you bothering about?'

'You—and Maureen. How is she?'

'Oh, she's great.'

'And the little girl?'

'She's all right.'

'I thought she'd been poorly.'

'She's all right, I tell you.'

'You're off duty now,' I said. 'Aren't you going home?'

'Later. What's it to you?'

'I thought Maureen might be glad to see you.'

He looked at me for a moment from eyes sick with pain. 'You don't *know* . . .' he muttered.

'Perhaps I know more than you think, Johnny. You're not home much these days—or nights—are you?'

'For Chrissake, leave me alone, will you?' he whispered.

'Where're you going now?'

'I've got an appointment.'

'At The Mainbrace?'

'So you've been poking your damned nose, have you?'

'Oh, for God's sake, Johnny, grow up—every man on the strength knows what you're doing to yourself. Don't you understand that you're on the way to the point of no return, that you're liable to smash your whole career?'

'I tell you I'm doing fine.'

'I'll tell *you* one thing for free, Johnny—you're drinking too hard and too often, your work's slipping and you're headed for a physical and mental collapse.'

He stared at me. It was like a silent snarl. All the engaging boyishness had vanished from his face—a face ravaged by the tell-tale signs of sodden indulgence.

'Good *night*,' said Johnny Dallas.

III

It took less than another year for Johnny to become the architect of his total disintegration. On a wild January night he walked into Headquarters, white and shaken, to tell me his marriage was finally in ruins. His young wife had left him, gone back to her parents for good with their baby girl. And Johnny? He was going out on duty reeking of booze. Not that it mattered—his 'duty' was another round of the dockland pubs and a night's kip at The Mainbrace.

But it didn't last. It couldn't last. The new D.I. liked to have young Jacks in his pocket, but he had no use for a man who was in the penultimate stages of disintegration. Drink, carelessness, a final inability to cope even with routine situations put him on the skids. His health cracking, he quit—taking his severance money with an alcoholic optimism about carving out a new career. The 'contacts' he knew so well along the waterfront would help him. Hadn't he been a bloody good friend to them?

Johnny Dallas, detective in the C.I.D. of one of the

great police forces in Britain, was indeed a good man to have on your side. But Johnny Dallas, ex-detective and maudlin drunk, meant less than nothing. The keepers of the waterfront bars and the ships' officers among whom he had once been hail-fellow-well-met had no use for him now. Johnny Dallas was no longer a friend at court.

His last remaining civilian friend was the faithful Benny Foy, the cruelly deformed lad who still worshipped him in spite of everything.

'Johnny'll get well and rejoin the police, Mr. Prendergast, you'll see,' he said.

'He was a good policeman, Benny,' I said, 'but not now. He's a good Jack who turned into a wrong Jack, you know that.'

Tears misted his pale blue eyes. 'I don't believe that, Mr. Prendergast—I'll never believe that, never,' he protested. 'Johnny's a good man, I tell you.'

I didn't try to argue with him. It was true that, fundamentally, Johnny Dallas was a good man—but he had this weakness for easy living. Yet it might never have engulfed him but for the influence of Frank Arnold. You need an indwelling toughness of character to resist the kind of soft temptations Arnold put in the way of men he wanted to use, and Johnny Dallas didn't have it.

But Benny Foy would not hear of this. He was the last true friend.

IV

Then, precisely at eleven o'clock on a Saturday night when sea fog was creeping coldly through the streets of the city, I went into the Information Room at Headquarters.

The girl radio announcer was putting out a message: 'Calling Z Victor One and Two. Proceed to Number 16a

Franklin Street. Man named Benjamin Alton Foy found dead in flat above Conn's jewellery store . . . believed shot . . . over and out.'

I ran out to the parking yard and drove there in my own car. I pulled up outside the shop simultaneously with the Z-car squads. A neighbour had heard a shot. A quavering grey-haired woman who lived next door. The shop was open and she went in and found Benny Foy. She was sobbing hysterically when we got to her.

'I'll never forget it . . . it was horrible . . .' The words tumbled from her.

I went in with the team. Benny Foy was sitting in a hide leather armchair, leaning far back. He didn't have a face. Most of it had been blown away with a .38 calibre revolver bullet. It had gone clean through his head. I found it on the floor behind the chair. It was murder all right.

I ran back down the stairs to the old woman. She was mumbling semi-incoherencies to herself. I took hold of her shoulders, tightly. The impact seemed to calm her.

'Did you see anyone near here after you heard the shot, love?'

She shrank back, as if I had said something that frightened her. 'It couldn't have been him,' she whispered. 'It couldn't have been him. They were friends, they'd always been friends.'

I felt a cold sag at my stomach. But I had to know. 'Who did you see?' I said harshly.

'It was Johnny . . . Johnny Dallas. He come out of the door after the shot. But they was friends, he'd never hurt little Benny, never . . .'

I let go of her. Jock Ewing came up. When he saw my face he stared. 'Bill— for Pete's sake, what's to do?'

'Johnny Dallas was seen leaving here after the shot was heard,' I said.

'Christ,' muttered Jock.

I drove back to headquarters. The D.I. wasn't in. He seldom was these nights. There were many social functions in the city and he liked to be seen at most of them. But, as it happened, the Chief Superintendent was there—an unexpected call on his way home from some engagement. I reported the circumstances without comment.

'Dallas.' There was no expression in his voice one way or the other. He eyed me levelly. 'You'd better bring him in for questioning.'

'About what, sir?'

The Super's eyes flickered. 'Murder,' he said. 'What else?'

'How about evidence, sir?'

'He was seen leaving that the shop immediately after the shot was heard. That calls for some convincing explanation.'

'It's possible Dallas might have called to see Benny Foy, sir. They were friends. He could have called and found him and gone after the killer.' Even as I spoke the words sounded flat.

'The woman didn't see anyone except Dallas, according to what you've told me,' said the Super. 'And if you're thinking the murderer left marks showing that he went out by the back way, why did Dallas use the front door?'

There was no answer to that and I didn't attempt one. Instead, I said, 'I don't believe Johnny Dallas shot him, sir. He isn't vicious, he's not the kind of man to kill anyone.'

'That's an expression of opinion,' said the Super coldly. 'We deal in facts, as you ought to know by now.'

'I know it, sir. I also know men. But, apart from that, what possible reason could he have for killing the one man who stood by him when his career and his private life fell to pieces round him?'

'You're asking *me* questions,' said the Superintendent.

'I'm sorry, sir.'

He looked directly at me. 'No, you're not,' he said. 'But, all right, I'll give you the answer. Dallas wrecked his career with the force. He became nothing more than a drunken layabout. A weak character. But a weak character, inflamed by alcohol, can brood on real or imagined grievances. Such a man can do unpredictable things, things normally out of character, perhaps not even understanding what he *is* doing. By your own account, Dallas left that shop within moments of the shot being fired. No one else was seen. The streets were empty . . .'

'There was fog, sir.'

'I know what you're suggesting—that some other person entered the shop unseen. But this old woman was watching. She couldn't have missed anything after she heard the shot. Those are the known facts. They are sufficient to hold Dallas for questioning—and I want you to bring him in personally.'

'Very well, sir,' I said. I went back to Z Victor One and told Jock Ewing where to drive. Johnny had a bed-sitter in a shabby cul-de-sac near Pitt Street in Chinatown. The room was a sea of chaos—unmade bed, gimcrack furniture bought from junk stores, jumbled toilet requisites on the cloudy glass shelf above a cracked wash-basin, old clothes strewn about the place. The air, or such of it as could get in through the dusty, ill-fitting windows, was thick with stale cigarette smoke and heavy with the reek of booze.

Johnny Dallas was sprawled on the bed, dirty, unshaven, ill—and almost paralytic drunk. It took more than an hour to bring him back to something resembling coherency. He remembered nothing.

'But I didn't shoot Benny,' he said. Why should I do it—why, why, tell me that.'

'You went to his flat, Johnny. You were seen leaving.'

He passed a hand across his wet forehead. 'I've been on the booze a week solid,' he answered. 'I haven't eaten everything except a few biscuits. I could have been anywhere in the last three days without knowing where. I was blacked out.'

'An old woman saw you leave. Can you remember her?'

'It's no use, Bill, I can't remember anything. I suppose you think I shot poor little Benny?'

'No,' I said. I thought of the sordid mess he had made of his life, a life that had promised so much. But I still had a duty to perform.

He got into the Z-car and sat staring dumbly at his hands dangling between his knees. 'I loved Benny,' he said at last. 'He was like a kid brother to me. Maybe I did kill him. I was so drunk I could have killed half a dozen men and not known what I was doing. But I'd never have done it consciously. For God's sake, you must believe that.'

'Yes,' I said. Something on his shabby jacket held my attention. It was a dullish stain. I knew what it was—blood. Less than thirty minutes later the lab men reported that the bloodstains were from Benny Foy's blood group.

It was an open-and-shut case.

We put Johnny in the cells. He made no protest, offered no comment. I walked slowly up the steps and into the big main room.

The Super came out of the inner room. 'We'll bring him before the court in the morning,' he said.

Frank Arnold, called from his home, was present now. 'It's Dallas all right,' he rapped. 'A disgrace to the profession. And a bitter disappointment to me personally because I gave him every chance of attaining promotion.'

Words jumped hotly into my mouth, but I had to leave them unspoken. I had something more to do than say what I thought about the power set-up at Headquarters . . . I had to prove Johnny Dallas innocent. I turned to the Super. 'We haven't found the murder weapon, sir,' I said.

Arnold shrugged. 'In the state Dallas was in he could have thrown it away without realising it, or even dropped it somewhere.'

'Perhaps, perhaps not.'

'What do you mean?'

'Just that I still don't believe Johnny committed this murder, sir.' I went from the room with their eyes boring into me. I had no clues, nothing to work on except the one thing that could not be given in evidence—an understanding of the nature of Johnny Dallas. Because, to me, this ruled him out, I had to look elsewhere. But suppose I was wrong, had missed some small significant thing in Johnny's make-up? I knew well enough that, given certain circumstances, men can do things inexplicable alike to themselves and to those with whom they are in the most intimate personal contact. I knew all this, but I also knew that Johnny Dallas had not killed Benny Foy.

The old woman who had heard the shot was a widow, a Mrs. Sarah Johns. She couldn't help me. The only person she had seen was Johnny—and she had watched the front of the store from the moment she heard the revolver fired. If anyone else *had* been there he must have left by the rear exit. It was possible because there was a short flight of stairs leading down to an alleyway. But this wasn't much to go on because there was no evidence that anyone had gone that way.

Then a thought occurred to me and I went to see Julius Conn. He lived across the Mersey at Egremont in a big rambling old house which he had kept on after his wife's death several years previously because, as he said, he could not bring himself to leave.

'These rooms are full of memories, Mr. Prendergast,' he said in his thin, slightly high voice. 'Some men want to forget their memories. I do not. My wife was everything to me, so I prefer to live in the place where my happiest memories were made.' He paused, then said evenly: 'I understand a man has been taken into custody in connection with this dreadful crime. What can I possibly do for you?'

'I don't think Dallas killed Benny Foy, Mr. Conn . . .'

He sat stiffly in an old upright chair, both hands clasped round the worn silver knob of a mahogany cane. 'Dallas is or was a police officer, a detective,' he said in a brittle tone.

'I know what you're thinking, Mr. Conn,' I rejoined, 'but it isn't like that. In fact, my superiors are convinced of his guilt.'

'Oh?'

'I'm not trying to prove Dallas is innocent because he was once a detective, but because I *believe* him to be innocent.'

He looked at me for a moment in silence. Then he said: 'I think you are an honest man, Mr. Prendergast. But even if this officer is guiltless I do not see what possible help I can offer.' He rapped the floor with his cane and the housekeeper came in. 'Would you bring two glasses of sherry, Mrs. Hancock?' he said. 'I like mine medium dry. And yourself?'

'The same, sir.'

'Ask me any questions you like,' Mr. Conn suggested.

'I have only one, Mr. Conn—to your knowledge did Benny Foy have any other friends?'

He shook his head. 'Benny found making friends difficult, for reasons which are not very creditable to other people, Mr. Prendergast. So far as I know, this man Dallas was his only close friend.'

'Relatives,' I pressed. 'Surely there must be relatives somewhere?'

'Well, he has a young sister.'

'I didn't know that, Mr. Conn.'

He shrugged. 'She lives with an aunt. A rather wayward girl, I am afraid. I know Benny was troubled about her.'

'In what way?'

'He thought she was, well, sexually wayward. Too fond of the boys—older men, too.'

'How old would she be?'

'Seventeen, at least I think so. She never visited Benny, though he used to call on her periodically—usually on Saturdays.'

Benny Foy was shot dead on a Saturday night. It was probably no more than coincidence, but I resolved to visit the little sister. Her name was Lucy and the aunt's house was in Beeker Street, in the heart of the 'B' Division of the Liverpool City Police, which is a very tough division indeed.

I went there at once. It was now 7.10 on a clear, cold night. The aunt, a Mrs. Jane Stokes, was out—but Lucy was in. A dark-haired girl with a pale painted face and a vaguely slack mouth. She was a looker all right, with a figure which would have made a deacon turn his head.

She opened the door to me and said: 'We're not buying anything tonight, see?'

I said patiently: 'I'm a police officer, a detective attached to the Criminal Investigation Department. May I come in for a few moments, Miss Foy?'

Her dark eyes blinked. 'Oh,' she said. 'Oh—you mean it's about Benny?'

'If you can spare a little time, yes.'

I went down a short dim hall and into a living-room heavy with overstuffed Victorian furniture, antimacassars, a glass-fronted cabinet full of china ornaments and presents from Blackpool. In the window a giant aspidistra fought an unequal battle for survival against the close musty air of the room.

'I don't know anything about what happened to Benny,' she said. 'I haven't seen him in two weeks.'

'I thought he dropped in on Saturday nights, Miss Foy.'

She fiddled with a brooch at the 'V' of her dress. 'Yeh, that's right, he came on Sat'days when he did come, but not lately.' She didn't look at me directly and I had a sudden, certain intuition that she was lying.

'Tell me about his last visit,' I said.

'He come two Sat'days ago, or was it three? I don't remember for sure.'

'What did he want when he came here?'

'Just to see me.'

'To see how you were getting on, you mean?'

'I suppose so. He . . .' She stopped.

'He was worried about you, wasn't he?'

She flared then. 'He was always pestering me, everlasting interfering with my life, that's what he was always doing. I tell you I got fair sick of it.'

'Why should he be worried, Miss Foy?'

She moved restlessly. 'How should I know?' she snapped.

'Well, if there was anything to worry about you would know what it was, wouldn't you?'

'Coming the older brother act, that's what he was always doing,' she muttered.

'Tell me about that,' I said.

She swung round, her face suddenly tight. 'I've told you,' she shrilled.

'Tell me again.'

'There's nothing to tell, except what I've just said and . . .' Her eyes swivelled to the door, but I was already going through it. I had heard the small sound, too.

I went fast down the hall and into the kitchen. A boy with overlong hair and a loose, sensual face wheeled as I came in.

'Who're you and what the bloody hell are you doing here?' he yelped.

'I was about to ask you that question,' I said.

He sneered. 'What's it to you, dad?'

'I'm a police officer investigating the murder of Benny Foy.'

His jaw slipped. Then he shrugged and said: 'So what? It's nowt to do with me, is it?'

'I don't know. What's your name?'

'Bert Collins.'

'Where do you live, Mr. Collins?'

'In Aiken Street.'

'What are you doing here?'

'I'm Lucy's boy friend,' he answered sullenly. 'Why shouldn't I be here?'

'And you come here when the aunt is out, eh?'

He glared defiance. 'Why not and what's it to do with you, copper?' he snarled.

'I don't know yet. I'm trying to find out. Did you know Benny Foy?'

'I've seen him once or twice, that's all.'

'Did he come on Saturday night or any time on Saturday?'

'How should I know?'

'You'd know if you were here when he called.'

'Well, I wasn't, see? I was out with me mates.'

'Benny thought his young sister was being promiscuous,' I said.

'Being what? Talk English, can't you?'

'He thought she was too fond of boys, especially as she's only seventeen.'

'Get lost!' Bert Collins grated.

'Being too fond of boys could include being too fond of you,' I went on.

'And if she was, what of it?'

'Nothing, at least nothing that's illegal. But it could have some bearing on this case, couldn't it?'

'How should I know?' he yelled. 'All right, I've been with her. I'm her boy friend. Benny didn't like it but he didn't like anything she did. Always coming round bleating at her and pestering her. The bloody little . . .'

'So you didn't like him?'

'No, I didn't and that's a fact.' His eyes suddenly narrowed. 'What are you trying to prove, copper?'

'Just at this time I'm not trying to prove anything. I'm in the process of trying to find a reason for what happened.'

'They've already arrested the fella what killed him.' Bert Collins said. 'I seen a bit in t'paper about this fella helping the police with their inquiries . . .' His heavy, sallow face twisted. 'I get it—you're trying to get this copper off the hook, that's what.' He wrenched the back door open and said: 'I'm off, see?'

'I'm not attempting to stop you,' I answered.

He half-turned with his hand on the door knob. His eyes flickered, first at me and then across the kitchen. He went out into the backyard, slamming the door violently. I yanked it wide open and went after him. He was going through the yard gate into the alley when I dropped a hand on his shoulder. He spun round, his face a mask of terror.

'I'll have it, if you don't mind, Collins,' I said.

'Wh . . . what?'

'The gun. A .38 calibre revolver. I imagine you've got it on you.'

For a tiny moment in time he stood utterly still, scarcely seeming to breathe, like a stone man. Then, without warning, he swept a hand down inside his sagging jacket. It was no more than a blur of motion, but he still wasn't quite fast enough. I brought my hand down in a hard chop. The impact nearly crumpled him. He made a sound, trying to lunge at an angle; but I had a police lock on him, thrusting his right arm downwards until another marginal pressure would have cracked the bone.

He made a small screech. 'Let go me arm, you're like to break it . . . for Chrissake let go!'

I slackened the pressure, but still kept the arm-lock on while I marched him back into the house. Lucy Foy was standing there. 'You've got my fella,' she wailed. 'You've got my Bert . . . it wasn't his fault . . . it was Benny everlasting harping and moaning and . . .'

Bert Collins yelled: 'Shut up, you nit!'

I took the lock off his arm, pushed him down into a chair and drove a hand inside his jacket. The gun was there, a .38 Smith and Wesson.

'It makes no difference now, does it?' I said. 'The joke's over.' I walked across the floor to the point where his eyes had flickered. In a drawer of the dresser there was a small box he hadn't had the chance to take with him when he ran out. Some cartridges were in it.

Bert Collins stared at the box, then at the gun. His lips moved, but for a moment nothing came. Then he broke. 'I killed him . . . the little crookbacked nosy,' he said.

'Coming between me and my Judy he was, always trying to . . .'

'Trying to stop you seducing her?'

Lucy Foy screamed: 'Whaddyer mean, you lousy Jack, you? Bert's had me a lot of times. I wanted him to, see? But our Benny had to come sticking his nose in . . .'

'He was trying to protect his sister,' I said. 'Does a man have to be murdered for that?'

I put Bert Collins in my car with handcuffs on him and drove back to Headquarters. Everything I had felt intuitively inside me was being vindicated. But, above all else, I was bringing the news that would save Johnny Dallas's life . . . and perhaps give him the chance to make a new and better one. I parked the car in the police yard, walked round to the main office with the prisoner. Sergeant Alderson and Constable Blake were behind the long counter. They looked up inquiringly.

Frank Arnold came out of his office. He started to nod towards me, then he saw Collins and an odd look moved on his face. 'What's this man in for?' he demanded.

'The murder of Benjamin Foy, sir,' I said.

It was as if I had struck him. He almost reeled back. 'What!' The word was like a parched rustle.

'I've formally charged him and he's admitted it.' I stared at Arnold's face. There was an expression on it which for a moment I couldn't analyse. Then, shatteringly, I knew. I stood there, waiting for him to tell me. It took him perhaps five seconds, but they seemed like an eternity.

When he finally spoke it was in a voice I hardly recognised. 'Dallas died in hospital twenty minutes ago.' He turned and walked back into his office. The door closed with a faint click. Alderson and Blake stood unmoving behind the counter.

Two men—one crippled in body and the other in

mind—had died. Why? I could not answer my own unspoken question. Perhaps there was no answer. I was oppressed, not for the first time, by the meaningless absurdity of life. Some men lived long, happy and untroubled lives. Some were trapped in the morass of human greed and frailty. A man could be struck down by a killer or by the cruel blows of illness while another, no better and no worse, escaped. Benny Foy never harmed anyone in his life, but he was dead. Johnny Dallas never willingly harmed anyone except himself and he was dead, too. There was no meaning, no pattern that made sense. There wasn't even anything you could say or do.

Quietly, Bert Collins began to sob. . . .

2

The Last Job

When I first knew Toby Varley he was fifty years old—a fine, well-built man with a broad smiling face and a soft burr in his deep voice. He had come to Liverpool from Birmingham, though Somerset was his native county. He was a kindly man who gave no trouble when he was arrested, and the records showed that he had been arrested three times in the last ten years. The count would no doubt have been higher but for the prison sentences he had had to serve.

It was Sam Goodyard, who had returned to Headquarters as Detective Inspector after Arnold had gone back to the regional organisation, who told me that Toby had taken up residence in our city.

'You'd better keep your beady eye on this fella, Bill,' he cautioned. 'I take it you know all about him?'

I nodded. 'Tobias Varley, king of the jelly men,' I said. 'I understand he has a very cunning way with a safe, even the strongest.'

Goodyard grinned. 'There may be a few safes, happen some in the Bank of England, this fella can't crack, but I wouldn't like to bet on it,' he said. 'The Super's been on the phone about Toby. He's anxious that we don't get caught napping.'

'Well,' I rejoined, 'we can't have him watched twenty-four hours of the day, and even if we work in shifts we can't hope to be right behind him all the time.'

'No, but we'd better put him under observation as far as possible,' the D.I. said. He tapped a file on the desk before him. 'This is a list of all businesses which are likely to have money on the premises. They're being asked to take special security precautions and those who have a habit of leaving money in safes overnight are being asked to use the banks' night safety-deposit system.'

'Well, that'll do for a start,' I said. 'Too many firms leave their takings on the premises all night.' I stood up and put my hat on.

'Going somewhere?' queried Goodyard.

'I think I'll chat Toby up a bit, Sam. Drop a kindly word in his shell-like, eh?'

'You mean tell him to behave himself or else.'

'It might do the trick, you never know,' I said, and went out.

Toby had taken a pleasant semi-detached house on one of the new estates out near the East Lancashire Road. It was shortly after ten o'clock in the morning when I called and he was reading a newspaper in the lounge overlooking a small, well-rolled lawn.

I liked him at once. There are those who say an honest citizen has no business taking a fancy to a villain, but life is not all black and white; there are many intermediate shadings . . . and even a villain can be likeable. Some, anyway.

'So the Jacks down in Brum have sent out a signal, have they?' he said. 'Well, Mr. Prendergast, they're wasting your time. I've retired.'

'On your ill-gotten gains, I suppose?'

'You could say that and I wouldn't argue with you,' replied Toby amiably. The corners of his mouth crinkled humorously. 'On the other hand, I wouldn't necessarily agree, neither,' he added carefully.

'Well, I'm not asking you to incriminate yourself about past misdemeanours,' I told him. 'I'd just like to feel that you aren't going to commit any new ones in our parish.'

Toby chuckled. 'Why, Mr. Prendergast, I just told you I've retired,' he said. 'My dear wife died some time ago and I've come here with my widowed sister Edna and my young daughter Mary. She's just started a new school here and will be taking her O-levels next summer.' His homely face lit up with pride as he spoke.

'I can see right away that you're very fond of your daughter, Toby.'

'For her I'd do anything,' he said simply.

'That's fine . . . just so long as it isn't anything you'd be ashamed to have her know.'

His eyes clouded. 'She knows I've been inside,' he said slowly. 'But all that's in the past now and I'm just going to live quietly and be a good father to her.' He glanced sideways as a footstep sounded. 'That's Edna, she's been out shopping. She'll make us some coffee.'

Edna Carter was a buxon women, perhaps seven or eight years younger than her brother She had the same unforced friendliness. I took to her on sight.

When she brought the coffee in Toby said: 'There's something in the paper, in the small adverts. I can't quite make it out.' He was holding the paper very close and had put on a pair of gold-rimmed spectacles.

'If you can't read it why don't you get your glasses changed?' I asked.

Edna Carter exclaimed: 'That's exactly what I keep telling him! He's been having trouble with his eyes lately.'

'All right, all right,' said Toby pacifically. 'I'll see the optician today, if it'll please you.'

'It's not a question of pleasing me but of safeguarding your vision,' his sister replied firmly.

Two and a half months went by without even a hint of trouble from Toby Varley. Even the Super was convinced that he had reformed. But though I had taken this personal liking to Toby, I was wary. The police have a saying about once a hook always a hook. This is not always true because hooks have been known to reform; but it seemed to me that more than a couple of months were needed before we could forget all about Toby Varley.

Summer, such as it was, came and went. The mellow mists of autumn were upon us when, at 9.40 on a mild October morning, Alderson put his head round the door of the C.I.D. room and announced; 'Break-in at Slazenby's warehouse, Bill. A jelly job— safe blown and four hundred pounds nicked.'

'Any clues?'

'Couldn't say. It's only just been reported on the phone by the manager. He's in a right state—especially after the warning to use the banks' night safes.'

'Are the boys out?'

'Z Victor One just going out. I thought you'd want to go with them.'

I nodded. Twelve minutes later we were there. The place had no night watchman and there were no private houses in the vicinity, so nobody had heard the muffled blast of the gelignite charge. It looked like an expert job —clean, neat and, I judged, quick. That didn't automatically implicate Toby Varley because there were three other known jelly men at large in the city, having completed their most recent sentences. I checked them first. They all had alibis. Crooks usually do have them, so that meant nothing. It's the honest citizen who often finds it difficult to account for all his movements during all the twenty-four hours of any given day.

Just the same, I had a feeling that for once the alibis

were genuine. That left me with Toby Varley. I drove out to the housing estate. There was no one in. A neighbour was peering through her net curtains, an inquisitive-looking woman well advanced in years. Every suburb has one like her.

I rang the bell of her house. There was a small delay before the soft pad of slippered feet sounded faintly in the hall. Then the door was open and I was looking at a slight figure wrapped in a shapeless dressing-gown of indeterminate colour.

'Do you by any chance know where Mr. Varley is?' I asked.

'They've gone off on holiday,' she said.

'Oh—when did they go?'

'This morning. Must have been sudden like because I never heard them say they was going.' She sniffed. 'I haven't had a holiday in three years and off they go in a hired car. Him and his sister and the girl. It's half-term for her.'

I said: 'How do you know it was sudden? They might have been planning it for months.'

'I heard the girl saying summat about it being a lovely surprise.'

'I see. You hear a lot of things, eh, Mrs. . . .?'

'Oakshaw, Mrs. Oakshaw. Who are you then? A friend of his?'

'You could say that. Do you happen to know where they've gone?'

She pushed strands of wispy grey hair off her forehead and nodded. 'I heard that, too. They've gone to Blackpool, that's where they've gone. Nice to be some people, I must say.' The old crone eyed me cunningly, looked past me to the Z-car I had come in. 'You're from t'police—that lot out there. What's he done then?'

I let it go. Instead, I said sardonically: 'You seem

very well informed. I suppose you don't also happen to know where they're staying in Blackpool?'

It was no more than a casual question, but she answered it triumphantly. 'I heard him tell t' driver. It's a hotel on North Shore.' She told me the name of the hotel and added with some bitterness: 'Going all that way in a taxi . . . must have tons of money.'

I drove up to Blackpool in my own car. Toby Varley wasn't in the excellent hotel he had checked into with his sister and daughter. I ran him to earth in the sun lounge on North Pier. He had £391 on him.

'It's me own money, Mr. Prendergast,' he said blandly. 'I told you I'd retired. You've nothing on me.'

'You don't need all that cash for a couple of weeks in Blackpool,' I said.

He made a fine, careless gesture. 'I like to go away well heeled,' he replied. 'Have a cigar.' He put a hand in his pocket and brought out a handsome case. Something fell from it. Instanly he put a foot on it. An unthinking reflex movement. If he had merely stooped to pick it up I might have thought nothing of the incident. But what had fallen out of the case was a small section of paper which had become wedged in the case after lying in his pocket. It turned out to be a piece ripped off a corner of a ledger in the warehouse safe . . . and it put Toby Varley behind bars for three years.

He bore no malice about it. To him it was the luck of the game. His sole worry was the effect it might have on his young daughter.

'I shouldn't have done it,' he told me, when they took him down from the dock at the Assizes. 'I had a little money—enough to live on quietly, like. But I just couldn't resist that safe. You see, I happened to know the warehouse had no watchman and it looked such a soft touch.'

'It would have been, too, but for that tell-tale bit of paper you missed,' I said.

He passed a hand across his eyes, screwing them up slightly. Then he said: 'Can I ask you something, Mr. P? Will you look in on Edna and Mary every now and then while I'm away?'

I gave him the promise and kept it.

Toby Varley was, as always, a model prisoner. He got his full remission and I drove his sister and daughter out to Walton to meet him on the day he was released. He had the greyish pallor you acquire in prison and looked older. I had expected that. It was something else about him that disturbed me. His sister had explained that he was having increasing trouble over his vision, but I had not been prepared for what I was now seeing: Toby Varley was nearly blind.

After that I used to meet them occasionally in one of the city parks—often it was just Toby and his daughter, now over seventeen, with her pet dog on a lead.

'You kept your word about looking in on Mary and I'll never forget that,' Toby said.

'Are you all right for money?' I asked him.

Mary smiled. 'Aunt Edna has a pension and I'm working now in an office,' she said. 'We haven't much to spare, but we manage and Daddy's happy.'

Then, one night when I was on Z-car patrol with Jock and Bert, something happened. We had turned off Mount Pleasant and were going down towards the Dock Road when I heard it—a dull sound like a distant explosion.

Jock, who was driving, said: 'It came from down there, somewhere down Tinling Street.' He set the cowled roof-light winking, made a right-hand turn and braked the car outside a supermarket.

There was a light coming from the basement, though the front entrance was locked. We ran down an entry along the side of the place and found an open door. The office was on the first floor. It was in a state of wild disorder.

'The safe's been properly jellied,' remarked Jock.

It certainly had. Some safe-blowers today use new types of plastic explosive, but this was a gelignite job. Yet only part of the safe had been blown and through the jagged hole you could see a tumbled mass of banknotes and coins. There was something wrong about the whole set-up. Articles were scattered all over the place—jemmies, a screwdriver, copper detonators, bits of plasticine, packets of chewing gum. And on the buckled door—blood.

Jock stared round. 'It looks like a three-handed or at least a two-handed job,' he said.

'Yes, that's what it looks like.'

He glanced swiftly at me. 'You said that in a funny sort of way,' he commented.

'Did I?'

'As if you had some other idea, Sarge. Happen you have?'

'Happen.' I examined everything, careful not to touch surfaces which would show fingerprints, though I felt pretty certain there wouldn't be any. Safe-blowers use rubber gloves as well as plasticine, chewing gum, wood tamps and knitting needles.

We were in the middle of it when footsteps sounded and a sallow man in a dark business suit came in. He stood on the threshold staring from one to the other of us.

'Are you the manager?' I asked.

'Er, no, I am the owner,' he said. 'Loring, James Loring.' He came further into the office and emitted a loud gasp. 'Great heavens, the safe has been interfered with . . .'

It seemed like a masterpiece of understatement.

'We heard an explosion and saw a light in the basement,' I said. 'I take it you were down there.'

'Yes, as a matter of fact. I was—ah—checking some new deliveries in the stockroom.'

'Didn't you hear the explosion yourself, Mr. Loring?'

'I did hear a sound, but I wasn't sure where it came from. Then, after a few minutes, it occurred to me to run upstairs and have a look round.' He nursed ringed fingers along the line of his thin jaw. 'I—er—must admit that I didn't hurry. To tell you the truth, I began to wonder if someone was upstairs and I was a bit scared. Fear of violence, you know.'

'Well,' I said, 'whoever did this job seems to have made a botch of it. There's still plenty of money in the safe, so far as I can see. Perhaps you can give us the exact financial position.'

Mr. Loring approached the safe gingerly, as if he expected it to bite him. Then he turned and said: 'Really, we shall not be able to say exactly how much has been taken until the door has been expertly removed and a detailed check made.'

'All right,' I grunted. 'We'll have someone round first thing in the morning. In the meantime, don't touch anything, sir.'

'I—ah—am not wholly unaware of the importance of not touching anything on the scene of a crime,' Mr. Loring intoned.

I walked into Headquarters at nine o'clock next morning just as the telephone rang. Alderson, who was now on day duty, said: 'Bill—here a moment. This'll interest you.' He wrote rapidly on a pad, put the receiver down and said: 'Toby Varley's dead.'

It stopped me in my tracks.

'The case has been reported to the Coroner, that's how we come into it,' Alderson said.

'You mean it wasn't a natural death?'

'Doesn't look like it. Apparently he was rushed to hospital last night bleeding from the mouth and told the doctors he had stumbled into a spiked railing. Hey—where are you off to?'

'The hospital,' I said.

The surgeon who handled casualty ward cases was young Ian Charters. I knew him well, had known his father before him.

'I understand Varley said he ran into a spiked railing or something,' I prompted.

The surgeon smiled. 'He did say that, though I don't see how he could be positive what it was because he was suffering from at least ninety per cent defective vision. Besides, apart from the gashes on his face there were traces of burning.'

'Could the burns be associated with any kind of explosive, Ian?'

'It's possible, though I can't be sure.' Young Charters eyed me closely. 'Why, what makes you ask?'

'It was just an idea I had, doctor. By the way, have you got his clothes?'

'The night sister will know where they are. Do you want to see them?'

'If sister doesn't object.' I thought for a second, then added: 'And even if she does . . .'

Charters chuckled. A few moments later I was looking at Toby's belongings. They included a donkey jacket with tapes stitched on the inside. Jelly men use tapes like this to hold jemmies and a screwdriver. In one of the pockets was an old tobacco tin. There were minute traces of gelignite in it. It was enough to make a charge stick. But Toby Varley was dead and there was no one to charge.

I got back into my car and drove out to the suburbs.

Toby's sister and daughter were there, with eyes red from weeping.

'Toby was a good man, Mr. Prendergast,' said Edna Carter.

'Yes. He was a criminal, but he was also in all other respects a good man. Not like some of the villains today.'

Mary touched my arm. 'Daddy was always good to me,' she said. 'Even when he came home with his face in such a terrible state he was good to me.'

'Oh?'

'We sent for the ambulance, though ke kept saying he'd be all right, but we could see he was badly hurt. Before they took him to hospital he gave me a present. He said he had intended giving it me in the morning—it's my birthday, you know, I'm eighteen.'

She took an envelope off the sideboard and showed it to me. Inside there was £250 in fives, held together in a wad by a wide elastic band. It could be money saved from the past, but I doubted it. Criminals, even kindly ones like Toby Varley, toss their money around. With them it's easy come, easy go, because they think there's always another job they can do.

I recalled that once, when I met him sitting in the park while Mary had walked off exercising her pet dog, he remarked that if he ever did another job it would be his last—but then only to leave something for the daughter he loved. 'But, of course, I'll never do it now, Mr. P,' he said in his soft burr. 'I'm on the straight and narrow now, eh?'

Perhaps he had meant to be. But good intentions are sometimes dissolved by circumstances, like inhibitions in alcohol. Toby knew his sight was going, so that time was running out for him. The money in the envelope could only be the proceeds or part of the proceeds of a raid bungled not because his skill had left him . . . but because he was virtually a blind man.

I was going to have to take that money off Mary Varley, but I didn't tell her there and then. It occurred to me that first I had better check the deficiency in the safe with Loring.

He was at his desk going through the books. It seemed to me that he looked slightly strung-up, like a man who hadn't slept too well. The safemakers had got the door right off and he had checked the contents.

'It's all there, intact—not a penny missing, Mr. Prendergast,' Loring said. His face was suddenly bland and smiling. But his eyes weren't.

'You're quite sure of that?'

'Quite.' He closed one of the books with a swift movement. 'The—ah—burglar must have been a very amateurish sort of person.'

'He was an expert named Toby Varley.'

'Really?' he looked politely uninterested.

'Toby Varley's dead,' I said suddenly.

A look flickered briefly in his eyes and was gone. Just a look that vanished so fast it might never have been there—but I had seen it. And his small inner tension vanished, too.

'I don't know anyone of that name,' he said carelessly.

I looked hard at him. 'If we hadn't heard the explosion we wouldn't have known all about this unless you phoned us, Mr. Loring,' I remarked.

'Well, it makes no difference, does it?' he answered smoothly. 'I mean I can account for every penny.'

'I'm sure you can,' I said drily.

I drove back to Police Headquarters. I knew Toby Varley had pulled his last job. So, perhaps, had somebody else.

3

Angel Face

When I walked into Sid Rose's pawnshop one fine morning in early spring I had no notion of the complex chain of events I was about to be called upon to unravel. The visit was simply one of a number I was making up and down the city—a laborious but purely routine check on all pawnbrokers on the chance that a £500 ring stolen in a housebreaking raid might have been pledged there.

I explained the situation to Sid Rose—a small, dark-haired young fellow with restless eyes and quick movements who had helped us on more than one occasion in the past.

'Know what you want, Mr. P,' he said tersely. 'I'll show you what I've got on hand.'

He spread all his pledged rings on a worn oblong of black velvet. I examined them carefully, checking details against the description I had brought with me. But the one I was after wasn't there and I was about to say as much when he said: 'Is that it?'

He pointed a cigarette-stained index finger at a slim gold ring set with diamonds and added: 'It's not five hundred nicker's worth, but it'd fetch two-fifty second-hand.'

I shook my head. 'No, it's not from my job, Sid.'

'Oh, well, in that case . . .' He started moving the rings.

I eyed him curiously. 'What made you think it might be?' I asked.

'Oh, it's nothing then . . .' He made a small shrug.

I leaned against the counter, still watching him. 'Sid,' I said slowly, 'there appears to be something on your mind and what I'm thinking is that you'd better tell me.'

He reached under the counter, brought up the dog-end of a cigarette, lit it and dragged the smoke deep down. His face wore a worried look.

'If that's not the ring you're trying to trace I don't see as it matters,' he said.

'You don't see that *what* matters?'

'Nothing . . .'

'Look,' I countered, 'something seems to be bothering you and it might save a lot of trouble later if you told me.'

He stirred uneasily. 'I don't know that I ought to say owt.'

I lit one of my own cigarettes and said: 'If it's anything that might conceivably involve the police at some stage it'll be better off your chest.'

'I don't want to cause trouble unnecessarily, Mr. P.'

'Then suppose you tell me what it is—in confidence? If it doesn't involve us in any way it'll stay under the hat.'

He took the cigarette from his mouth and looked at it, as if trying to make up his mind. Then, abruptly, he said: 'I'm not sure, only . . . well, that particular ring was brought in by a woman, a very well-dressed young woman with a real nice voice, educated you might say. I mean she must be all right, only . . .'

'Only you're not sure and because of that you're a bit worried?'

'Well, yes, as a matter of fact I am. You see, when she came in my shop I had a funny sort of feeling she'd been in before. Mind you, she didn't appear to know me from Adam and at first I thought I must've got her mixed up with someone else.'

'But, just the same, you took the ring in pawn,' I said.

'Yeh, I took it. There wasn't any reason why I shouldn't, was there?'

'And it was a satisfactory deal, eh?'

'Well, it was just in the way of business, Mr. P.'

'Of course,' I replied. What I was thinking was that his desire to make a good business deal had overcome any feeling he had about fancying that he'd seen the customer before. Jewellers and pawnbrokers are shrewd operators when it comes to turning a profit . . . and if a person pawning a £250 ring can't find the cash to redeem it after twelve months the pawnbroker nets a very nice profit indeed by putting it in the annual sale.

I said as much to Sid Rose.

A faint grin came on his friendly features. 'Well, that's business, ain't it?' he argued.

'Yes, it's business, unless . . .' I let the last word fall heavily.

The grin ebbed. Anxiety took its place 'Business is one thing, but stealing is something else. You don't think . . .?'

'You can set your mind at rest,' I told him. 'So far as I know, we've no record at Police Headquarters of this particular ring having been stolen.'

'Oh!'

'I've already suggested as much, so what's worrying you?' I asked.

He ground the remains of his cigarette out in a loaded copper tray and said slowly: 'After I took this ring in I still kept thinking I'd seen her before. I was bloody sure I knew her and yet somehow I just couldn't remember when or where.'

'All right, so you had a bit of after-wit,' I said. 'What did you do about it—if anything?'

'Well, she said she was a Miss Janet Carstairs—and that certainly wasn't any name on my books.'

'You must have been misled by a chance resemblance to someone else.'

'No. The more I thought about it the more I felt sure. It was at t'back of me mind for days, it fair bothered me.'

'Go on,' I said quietly.

'She left her address and a phone number and I rang the place up,' Sid said. He looked at me and added flatly: 'Nobody of that name lives there, Mr. P.'

'Odd,' I mused.

'That's what I thought, and yet . . .' He spread both hands in a gesture.

We not only had no report in about the ring he had shown me—but we had no information of any kind about a well-dressed and well-spoken young woman answering to the description of the one who had pledged it. Yet, quite suddenly, I had an intuitive feeling that I was on to something.

'Of course, there may be nothing in it,' Sid was saying.

'Will you let me borrow that ring while I try to find out its history?' I asked.

'Sure, that's all right, Mr. P.' He spread the velvet oblong out on the counter again.

I gave him a receipt and took the ring to one of the major experts in the city. Rings carry the jeweller's mark on the shank, and he hadn't been peering at it through his magnifying lens for more than a few seconds before he looked up with a curious expression on his face.

'This ring belongs to our branch shop in Birkenhead,' he said.

'You mean they had it there in stock?'

'That's right.'

'They must have sold it, then.'

'I imagine so. Still, that's where it came from and that's what you wanted to know, isn't it?'

'Something like that,' I agreed. 'What I'm more interested in is who bought it.'

He looked puzzled. 'There's nothing illegal in someone buying a ring,' he ventured.

'Nothing whatever. It's just an enquiry which might have a bearing on something.'

He eyed me as if he were about to press the subject, but he didn't. He merely said: 'If it'll help, I could ring up our branch.'

'No, don't bother,' I said. 'I think I'll go over there.'

'Well, I'll tell them to expect you.'

'It's not necessary, but you can do it if you wish,' I answered.

I went straight away, taking my place in the seemingly endless queue of traffic pouring through the Mersey Tunnel. I was supposed to be still making the rounds of the pawnshops and the D.I. might reckon I was wasting valuable time . . . but I still had that intuitive feeling. I had had similar feelings on cases in the past and they had rarely led me astray. Even so, I wasn't prepared for the whole series of surprises which awaited me across the river.

The branch shop was just off the Borough Road, close to the town centre. The manager, a plumpish fellow in his early fifties named Frank Bradshaw, had already been told over the telephone that I was calling—but apparently he had little or no details.

I got the ring out and laid it on the shop counter. He took only one look at it and then said incredulously: 'But . . . but this is in stock . . . it's on display. Well, I mean it's supposed to be.'

'It isn't though, is it, Mr. Bradshaw?' I commented.

He yelled for the sales assistant. A slightly built young fellow with an alert manner bustled forward from somewhere in the back of the place.

'Yes, sir—did you want me?' he asked.

Bradshaw pointed to the ring. 'I didn't know this had been sold, Len,' he began.

'Heck, I'm sorry, Mr. Bradshaw,' the assistant said. 'But it was some days ago and you were out and I forgot to mention it. Why . . . is anything the matter?'

Bradshaw looked inquiringly at me.

'Can you tell me who bought it?' I asked.

Len looked uncertain and the manager cut in: 'It's all right. This is Detective Sergeant Prendergast from Liverpool . . . he's making some inquiries. You're at liberty to tell him anything you know.'

'It was a young woman, sir—a very well-dressed and superior sort of young woman, I'd say.'

'Describe her to me, will you?' I could have given Sid Rose's description but if I had Len might have imagined points of resemblance. It's invariably better to let the witness do his own describing.

'Lemme see,' Len reflected. 'About five feet five in her shoes and they had high heels. Aged twenty-eight or even thirty, no more. Fair hair, blue eyes, one or two small freckles. Wearing a powder-blue twopiece suit with a white silk or nylon blouse and a crimson scarf loosely knotted. White shoes, tan stockings—oh, and she had gloves, but she was carrying them, not actually wearing them.'

'I suppose she didn't have a long white scar on her left thigh?'

He flushed slightly. 'If that's a joke . . .' he began.

'It was meant as a compliment,' I said. 'On your powers of observation, I mean.' The description not only matched the one Sid had provided but had sketched in some more identifiable detail.

Bradshaw said interestedly: 'Can I inquire exactly what the point of all this is?'

'No reason why not—this ring was pledged with a pawnbroker in Liverpool.'

'What!' The manager wheeled on the hapless Len. 'Did you let her have it on appro?' he roared.

'She paid thirty-five pounds deposit, Mr. Bradshaw,' the assistant said. 'I acted in good faith . . .'

'Your touching faith is going to cost the firm plenty,' growled Bradshaw. 'Well, no, that's not right, is it? The ring's here. Just the same . . .'

'It seemed all right, Mr. Bradshaw, I'd no reason to think anything wrong. Besides, she knew all the nobs for miles around . . .'

'I stared. 'She *what*?'

'Well, we were chatting of this and that and she let fall a lot of names, well-known people in local society—that sort of thing. Besides, she had a real crocodile-skin handbag and a wallet stuffed with money. I saw it.'

'And so you let her walk out with a two-hundred-and-fifty-pound ring on a thirty-five-quid deposit?' I said.

'We've done it before, sir, if the customer looked all right . . . and she certainly did. A real lady I took Miss Marcroft for . . .'

'Miss Marcroft?' I echoed. 'The name she gave when she pawned the ring was Miss Carstairs.'

'Boody hell!' Len moaned.

'Did she say why she wanted the ring?'

'Aye—if it's true.'

'Never mind about that. Tell me what she said.'

'Something about her young sister being twenty-one in a week or two and that she wanted the ring for a present. She wasn't quite sure it was the right kind and wanted to take it home to consult with her mother. I tell you, nobody ever looked more genuine . . .' His voice trailed away unhappily.

'An address,' I said. 'Did she give an address?'

'Oh, yes. She said it was her mother's home and that she lived there. The mother's a widow. They're on the phone—she gave me the number.' He repeated it.

I turned to the manager. 'Do you mind if I use your phone?'

'Not at all. Go ahead.'

I called the number there and then and the result was like the one Sid Rose got—nobody of that name lived there or was known there.

That left me precisely nowhere, but something stirred far down in my mind, something that might provide a clue, even if a slender one. I went back to Liverpool and saw George Allison, the managing director of the company which owned the shops I had visited and a number of others. I described the young woman again, marshalling every remembered detail of appearance, clothing and manner as they had been given to me. It was no more than a chance, but before I had finished I knew it meant something to him.

'I've seen someone like that,' Allison said definitely. 'As a matter of fact, it was at some social occasion in the Town Hall. She was chatting with a little group of people at the refreshment buffet.'

'You met her?'

He shook his greying head. 'No, we weren't introduced, so I didn't get the name, but your description fits pretty accurately.'

I now had more than a hunch that I was on to something; I was certain of it. During the next few days I called on the number of jewellers, making a kind of cross-section of the trade in a wide area of the city. By weekend I had established a constantly recurring pattern. Over a period of several months a young woman, aged twenty-eight to thirty, with shining golden hair and wide-open blue eyes, had called at three-quarters of the shops I visited. Each of the managers was impressed not only by her looks and figure but by the quiet air of good breeding and unostentatious luxury which hung about her like an aura. Above all else, they were impressed by what one of them called 'the almost angelic saintliness' of her face.

The story related to me by Alexander Leeming, one of the store managers, was characteristic.

'She came in one morning and bought a ring for thirty pounds, paying cash,' he recalled. 'About a week later she returned with the ring and told our sales lady that she would like something rather more superior, something in the two hundred to three hundred pounds class. Well, naturally, my assistant was charmed to show her what we had to offer.'

Mr. Leeming paused to flick a speck of dust from the lapel of his beautifully cut suit and went on: 'I should explain that my assistant had taken note of her clothes, her manner, and not least, the fact that she had a wallet well provided with money. She let fall the information that she was shortly expecting considerable money from an inheritance. Oh, and the second time she called she dropped a small leather-bound book, like a diary. It fell open on the counter and the assistant could not help seeing that it was, in fact, an engagement book . . .'

Again the manager paused and when he resumed it was with that slight increase of intensity which comes to a man approaching the nub of a subject.

'Mr. Prendergast, the book was literally crammed with names,' he said impressively, 'extremely well-known names in this city.'

I smiled thinly. 'And she dropped it accidentally, eh?'

'Well, there was no reason to think otherwise,' Mr. Leeming replied. 'However, the point is that she chose several rings and seemed unable to make up her mind which one to settle on. Finally, she asked if she could take several on approval—after paying a deposit, of course.'

He gazed at me solemnly and resumed: 'She explained that she was a relative of the Reverend Oliver Shard and was, in fact, residing at the vicarage. She talked at some small length about her work for the Church Missionary Society and the youth club attached to the church. She even gave us the telephone number to ring if we deemed it necessary to check. But, of course, we didn't. It would have seemed like an impertinence.'

'The young lady would appear to be a gifted student of psychology,' I murmured.

'Perhaps. But everything seemed to be in perfect order. Indeed, our assistant suggested that she should take four rings each valued at approximately three hundred and fifty pounds. After a few days she brought three of them back and inquired if she could retain the fourth a little longer while she discussed the matter at home. We agreed —after all, she had returned the other rings, and we had her deposit as an act of good faith.'

'But this time, the last time, she hasn't come back, Mr. Leeming?'

'Not yet, no—but we felt fully justified in trusting her,' said Mr. Leeming.

I sighed. Getting a ring on approval after paying a £30 deposit was no crime. That could arise only if the ring had subsequently been sold elsewhere, and at this stage I had no evidence that it had been.

But I soon got it . . . and slowly the whole complex plot began to unfold like a film on a screen.

From shop to shop I went, and everywhere the story

was the same in all essential details. Rings, each one of them valuable, taken on approval, some returned but always one of them retained on some pretext or other . . . and each retained ring either pawned or sold outright at another and distant shop.

But I still had not the smallest clue to her identity. The Reverend Shard knew her all right, but as Martha Ackroyd. Four other vicars and as many curates knew her as Frances Ilkeston, Lydia Meredith, Olive Gray and Alice Fenton. At various times she had attended their services, had taken part in parish activities and had seemed not uninterested in such matters as altar cloths and chalices—especially the latter.

One worried clergyman said: 'She was interested in everything to do with our church. Indeed, she even asked where we obtained our chalices . . . the names of the jeweller's shop and all that kind of thing.'

'Yes, vicar,' I said grimly.

'And she knew such nice people, Mr. Prendergast. Prominent people, you know. Not just dropping their names.'

This was intriguing. 'How can you be sure of that?' I asked.

'Both my curate and myself have observed her in conversation with influential and responsible citizens. At various civic and other events, I mean.'

'I think you had better give me some of those names, vicar,' I said.

'Yes—yes, of course.' He shook his head, as if unable or unwilling to credit that there could possibly be anything wrong.

'We were quite distressed when she ceased coming to our church,' he added. 'Such a charming and unassuming person. She always referred to her young sister and, very particularly, to her mother. She had private means and I believe there was an inheritance due.'

I nodded without telling him that the inheritance had too often been mentioned by her to the jewellers she had coolly hoaxed. When I left I called on several of the influential and prominent citizens, but the result was as I had feared—they merely knew her by the false name she used.

The deeper I investigated the more intricate the whole thing became. I realised that she must have compiled a formidable index of jewellers and pawnbrokers, obtaining rings on approval from the one and pledging them with the other—a meticulously careful list so that she would not double back on her tracks. It was also clear that she must have written down a list of false names and addresses for herself, plus a detailed inventory of the socialite section of the community, complete with notes on their status and personal idiosyncrasies, so that she could bring up these telling little points in her charming and unassuming conversations.

But it has been well said that liars need long memories—and in the end she made her first slip, by going to two shops owned by the same company. True, she would be unaware of the joint ownership, but it was her business to know and she hadn't.

Well, every villian—even those with angel faces—finally makes a mistake. Even so, I was still as far off as ever from knowing who she really was. And now, after months of complicated 'deals' which had put a total of more than £4,000 into her genuine crocodile-skin handbag, she was no longer around.

'You know what's happened,' grunted Detective Inspector Sam Goodyard. 'She's made a nice fortune and now she's quit.'

'It's possible,' I assented, 'but we don't *know* that.'

'That's true. She could just be lying low for a while.'

The D.I. looked at me. 'You don't think she's got wind that you're on this job, do you?' he asked.

'I'd doubt that, Sam. The only people who could tell her are the jewellers and pawnbrokers—and the parsons. And I've asked them all to phone me if she shows up anywhere.'

'H'm.' Goodyard rubbed his chin reflectively. 'Well, one way and another there's a tidy sum involved and we ought to do something about it. All right, stay on the case and see what you can turn up.'

The prospects didn't seem promising. Then, late one dismal wet afternoon, I went into an obscure pawnshop in one of the poorest and toughest areas of the city. It was the slenderest of chances, for everything I had been able to build up in my mind about her scarcely suggested that she was the kind of young woman likely to enter that kind of shop.

You never can tell, though. For a detective there is only one infallible rule—never leave anything, however improbable, undone.

The shop was in a narrow street of decrepit terraced houses aching for paint, second-hand wardrobe dealers, dispirited fish-and-chip parlours and grim-looking Victorian pubs. Albert Needy had his frowsy pawnbroking establishment about half-way down the street.

He was short and grossly fat, so that he looked almost as wide as he was tall. Albert was also totally bald—and, to heighten the oddness of his appearance, he had no eyebrows. But the eyes which raked you were as cold and calculating as a computer.

Still, the law had had no trouble with him and I knew Albert wanted none. His clients were mostly poor or alternating between poverty and small tempory bouts of financial well-being. Some were door-to-door dealers in cast-off clothing, often ranging over considerable distances in search of the basic materials of their trade. They always wore either a valuable ring or a necklace of old sovereigns which they pledged with him when trade was bad. Nearly all this class of dealers wear quite costly rings; they call them their 'stock', which is a way of saying it is something they can fall back upon when things get a little difficult.

Yes, it seemed a forlorn hope that anyone so well dressed and well spoken as the unknown women I was hunting would go to Albert Needy's little corner shop, but I called there just the same. It was as well that I did.

There was a customer in the place when I entered, a woman. But by no stretch of the imagination could anyone have supposed she was the mysterious lady with the angelic face. She looked about a hundred years old, though she was probably pushing seventy, and had probably seemed old for the last thirty years. It is a curious fact, and one which hardly ever seems to be written about, that the working class as a group, and the poorer section in particular, age rapidly once youth has been passed; there seems to be scarcely no period of transition, of growing old by degrees.

The old woman shambled out, a shawl over her head, clutching a ten-shilling note in a veined hand.

From behind the counter, Albert wheezed: 'She allus pawns t'same thing, redeems it come Friday night ready to pawn again. I've a few like her.' His shrewd eyes darted at me appraisingly. 'Well, what can I do for the t'police Mr. P?' he asked.

'It's an odd sort of story,' I said. 'I'd better tell you pretty well all of it and then we'll see if you know anything.'

He listened without interruption and without any definable expression on his vast moon-like face, but I sensed his interest just the same. I had a notion that I had erred in not coming to Albert Needy earlier. Nor was I wrong.

'A young woman looking just like you say pawned a ring here,' Albert said.

'She did?'

'Yeh, that's right. A very posh Judy to come in a shop in this part of town.'

'When?'

'It weren't no more'n a week or ten days ago. I can get the date from me book. She give her name and address, too.'

'I don't doubt it,' I said sourly. 'She gives names and addresses all over the place and they're all phony ones.'

He shook his hairless dome. 'No, it weren't like that, Mr. P.'

'Oh, how do you know it wasn't?'

He grinned in a long thin line, showing no teeth though he had them. 'I checked the voters' list and it's there all right, a Birkenhead address.' He rummaged in a drawer, then shoved a scrap of paper across the counter. On it was scrawled in indelible pencil, the name *Suzanne Worley*, followed by a street address.

'You should've been a cop, Albert,' I told him.

'A cop—who, me? I wish you'd give over, Mr. P.'

'Well, running a swanky shop in the best part of town, then.'

'I make out all right,' he said.

I thought of all the high-class jewellers who had accepted her false names and addresses at face value on the strength of an angel face and probably acquired culture in her voice while a scruffy little pawnbroker in one of the lowest quarters of the city had been sharp enough to check against the voters' list. Of course, men like Albert Needy spend pretty well their whole lives dealing with the flotsam and jetsam of low life—and few things are more calculated to sharpen the wits and the instinct for self-preservation.

But why on earth had Suzanne Worley given him her real name? Perhaps she had run out of inventing false ones. Much more probably, success was making her careless—or she thought no one would ever contact a seedy shop like Albert's. Whatever the reason, she had at last betrayed herself.

Bert Rawlings drove me through the Tunnel to Birkenhead in a Z-car, moving up the Borough Road and then weaving through a number of smaller streets until we came to a quiet cul-de-sac and finally stopped outside a large, older-type house with double bays.

Instead of going straight up to the house, I decided to watch—there was the chance that she had been out on another job and might return with something on her that could be used in evidence.

Hours passed and nothing happened except that an elderly woman opened the front door and took an order off the grocery boy. There was no sign of a young well-dressed woman with shining golden hair and I began to wonder whether we were on the right track after all.

In the end I knocked on the door and the elderly woman stood there. She was probably sixty years old—and, seen close up, bore a clear resemblance to the description we had. She looked like a much older Suzanne Warley.

I explained that I was a police officer making some inquiries and asked if she was the occupier.

'Actually, I'm the owner, sir,' she replied. 'What can I do for you?'

'It's just an enquiry were making in the district,' I said. 'Is there anyone else in the family, Mrs. Worley?' I wasn't even certain that this was her name, but she nodded.

'I have a daughter,' she added. 'She doesn't live here,

though. She's a matron at a big hospital in the Midlands.' Her faded eyes lit up with pride as she spoke. 'Suzanne is a very good daughter, sir. She sends me money regularly and visits me regularly, too. Do you wish to speak to her?'

'Well, perhaps if you gave us the name of the hospital?'

'She'll be home this weekend, sir. In fact, I'm expecting her tonight. She always comes on a Friday night when she comes home.'

'Thank you,' I said. 'Perhaps if we came back later, eh?'

Actually, we hung around in the parked car, just off the street but within sight of the house. Almost on the stroke of eight a car drew up and a girl got out. The moment I caught sight of her I knew my search was over.

Then another woman followed her out of the car, though for an instant I thought it was a man. A tall, rangy woman with angular features and mannish clothes. Bert sent the police car forward and I got out and followed them up the path to the house.

I explained that I was a police officer making inquiries about a number of valuable rings and that I had reason to believe Miss Suzanne Worley could help in the investigation. Immediately, the mannish woman took charge.

'Anything you have to say you can say to me,' she snapped. 'I shall speak for my very dear friend and I shall consult my solicitors on her behalf.'

'Who are you?' I asked.

'My name is Alison Grayling and . . .'

'Well, Miss Grayling, are you trying to tell me that you know all about your friend?'

'I don't know what you mean.'

I took Suzanne Worley's left hand and held it up. On one of the fingers was a three-stone diamond ring. It was worth several hundred pounds. It was also one of the rings on the list I had been accumulating. 'I've come for that, among other things,' I said.

Suzanne Worley turned her angelic face towards me. Her eyelids drooped defensively. 'If you want my ring then indeed you must take it,' she murmured.

'It's not a question of my wanting it, Miss Worley. The question is where did it come from?'

She dabbed her wide blue eyes with a small cambric square. 'Oh, dear, I do hope there will be no trouble,' she said.

Alison Grayling was looking hard at her. 'What have you been doing, Suzanne?' she asked. 'Please tell this officer and myself where you obtained the ring, dear.'

'She gets them all over Liverpool and Birkenhead on approval and then pawns them, Miss Grayling,' I interrupted.

'What! I cannot believe it—say it isn't true, Suzanne,' Alison Grayling cried.

Suzanne Worley, smiled her beautiful angelic smile. 'But of course it isn't true,' she answered. 'Do I look like a dishonest person?'

'That's part of the trouble—you don't,' I said.

We drove them both to Police Headquarters, Alison Grayling having insisted on accompanying her friend. In the interviewing room I began the interrogation—and never, in a career during which I have had to confront some of the most plausible rogues of the underworld, had I ever encountered so fluent and convincing a liar as Suzanne Worley. Listening to her gentle, cultured voice and looking at her sweet, composed face would have convinced anyone—except perhaps a Jack with a naturally suspicious mind, which means all Jacks. She parried every question, turned every implication inside out, presenting a kind of immovable innocence as she sat there clutching her crocodile-skin handbag.

All the time she never let go of it for an instant, but for more than an hour I made no comment.

Then, suddenly, I said: 'Give me that bag, please.'

She shrank back, but I took the bag and upturned it on the desk between us. Eleven pawn-tickets cascaded out. For what seemed like minutes she sat there staring down at them. Then, at last, she broke.

Now I had the full story—more fantastically tangled than even I had suspected. For upwards of a year she had carried on a mounting series of manipulations which were to take me many more weary days and nights to trace back to their starting-points. I had to find the rings she still had hidden, the rings on which deposits had been paid and which had since been pledged—often in other cities and towns—and, above all, those which had been sold outright. Literally dozens of rings were involved and as many false names and addresses. At one point I was almost in a flat spin trying to find out where some of them had gone.

Finally, we booked her on fourteen charges of stealing, with another admitted twenty to be taken into consideration. Then, when the story broke in the newspapers, I was virtually inundated with telephone calls from shops all over the place—for now it transpired that Suzanne had also done a profitable line of business in twenty-two-carat gold wrist-watches on the side. The final sum involved ran into many thousands.

Of course, she never was a hospital matron. That was a tale she told her rather simple and devoted mother. Thousands of pounds had gone into Suzanne Worley's crocodile-skin handbag—yet when we caught up with her she was practically penniless. All the money had gone on high living in London—theatres, the best restaurants, custom-made clothes, cars, trying to mix with people in the upper bracket of London Society.

Alison Grayling, who had supposed her to be well-to-do and knew nothing of what had been going on, stood by her friend to the last. And so, indeed, did the vicars of the churches she had attended on her many trips home. Several came forward to testify to her good character in court. For them all the biggest shock was the discovery that all the time the angelic Suzanne had been weaving a tangled web of deceit and dishonesty . . . and even then they felt impelled to speak for her.

The Assize judge sent her to prison for eighteen months—and years were to slip by before I saw her again.

Then, one brilliant summer's afternoon shortly after my retirement from the C.I.D., I was walking down Lime Street when a well-groomed woman touched my arm and a remembered soft voice said: 'Well, Mr. Prendergast, I have often wondered if I would ever see you again . . .'

It was Suzanne. Still looking young and charming—and prosperous.

'I see you are writing for television,' she said. 'I'm a real fan, you know. In a funny sort of way I feel that I'm part of it when I see your name.' She smiled, the same angelic smile I recalled so vividly. 'But they don't seem to get away with it as long as I did,' she added.

'Well,' I grinned, 'you had a head start.'

'I did, didn't I? But that's all over now.' She pushed a strand of her shining golden hair off the pale oval of her face. 'I'm sure you will be so pleased to know that I'm now the personal secretary to the managing director of a very big company down south. It's such a wonderful position. I'm just up on another of my visits to Mother, you know.'

I looked at her, reflecting that she could talk her way into almost anything, just as she had exploited the gullibility of some jewellers and pawnbrokers whose eagerness to show a fast profit and even to drive a hard bargain had clouded their caution, so that the bigger the money involved the less care they seemed to take.

My face must have betrayed something of my thoughts because she touched my arm impulsively and said: 'It's all right, Mr. Prendergast. I really *have* finished with the past. I still don't truly know what made me do it, except that I wanted all the good things of life. Now I'm able to have them without my conscience troubling me.'

'I'm glad, Suzanne.'

'You know,' she said musingly, 'I have often wondered how you first managed to get on my track all those years ago.'

'It was just chance at first, then hard work and never giving up,' I rejoined.

I looked at her again, for the last time. She was wearing a very expensive two-piece in soft pink and, because it was hot, no gloves. On one of her exquisitely manicured hands a diamond ring glistened in the sunlight.

She saw me looking at it and smiled her angelic smile. 'Please do not worry, Mr. Prendergast,' she said. 'I bought that with money I earned.'

'In London, you mean?'

She laughed mellowly. 'Oh, no—I bought it at Mr. Bradshaw's charming little shop,' she said. 'He was *so* pleased to see me again . . . when I paid him in cash!'

4

The Confession

One of the dangers every policeman must be on his guard against is cynicism. This is not easy because you see so much that is ugly and mean and even brutal that something of it can brush off on to you, with a warping effect on your whole attitude to life.

But you have to fight it off—first because it is a bad thing in a personal sense and secondly because it will prevent you from observing and deducing objectively. Something else—it will destroy the springs of compassion, and they are vital. For although the darker side of human nature is not a pleasant thing there is a better side and always I have tried to see it.

Believe me, it does exist. Even in some though not all the tearaways. What I am trying to say in this true story is that love can purify a man. I know, because it reformed Albert Bright.

Like Toby Varley, he was a 'jelly man', an expert safe-breaker who knew, down to the final mathematical refinement, exactly how much gelignite was needed to blast open a steel door with safety, and how to handle this extremely dangerous explosive.

Before he was sentenced to five years in prison Albert had married a pleasant-looking and respectable girl named Joyce, to whom the revelation of his police record came as a shattering blow. She had had no inkling of it;

to her Albert was a quiet and affectionate man who was not dependent on his modest job as a storekeeper because he had modest private means inherited from the prudence and forethought of his late father. In fact, Albert's private means were exceedingly private—deriving wholly from nocturnal expeditions as a safe-blower only a few degrees less talented than the late Toby Varley, that supreme old supremo of the felonious art.

But deep though the shock of discovery was, she stood by him—and there was no doubt about the genuineness of Albert's love for her. He was twenty-four when he was sent down and when he came out he had only one aim: to go straight for the sake of the girl he loved and for the child she had borne him—the small son who, until the morning of his release, he had never seen.

For the boy was a Mongol. Joyce had never been able to bring herself to reveal this on her visits to the prison. When Albert saw the boy for the first time he felt that in some way it was a judgment on himself; that the boy's condition was due to the shock Joyce had suffered when, in her pregnancy, she first leaned of her husband's criminal background. More than ever now, Albert determined to abandon his past life.

But going straight is not always easy for such men. And for Albert Bright it was harder than for many. He had gone around with the Violet Gang, a bunch of tearaways led by a huge, granite-faced man called Ned Purdy whose fondness for flashy suits and violet-hued shirts gave the gang its fancy name. Shortly after Albert came out of jail they were waiting for him. By this time Albert was indeed going straight, working as a lorry driver.

He had just come off duty and was walking home when, as he came level with a transport café off the Dock Road, a voice said: 'Hi, Albert.'

Purdy was standing in the doorway of the café with the gang crowding behind him.

'Hello, Ned . . .' Even as he spoke Albert felt a cold sag at his stomach, a premonition of what was to follow. Since his release he had deliberately avoided all contact with his former associates and had begun to think they had finished with him. Well, perhaps they had; perhaps this was no more than a chance meeting. But Ned Purdy's next words dispelled that illusion.

'Come in and have a coffee with us, kid,' said Purdy. A smile cracked his hard face, but there was no smile in his brilliant eyes.

'In a bit of a hurry, Ned . . . going home,' muttered Albert. He hesitated, then resumed his stride.

A ham-like hand descended on his shoulder. 'Why, Albert, you ain't thinking of passing your old pals without a friendly chat, are you?' asked Ned.

'The wife'll wonder where I've got to,' said Albert.

'Quite the married fella, eh?' grinned Ned. 'Well, we'll not keep you only a few minutes. Got something to tell you, Albert.'

'Just a few minutes, then,' said Albert curtly.

'Sure, come right in, kid.' Ned led the way into the café. When they were seated round a coffee-stained table in a corner he said: 'You all right, Albert?'

'Not so bad.'

'You'll be better now you're home and not having to eat that bloody prison scoff, eh?'

'Yeh.'

'Thought you might've looked us up when you came out,' said Tiny Harker. He was a roly-poly of a man with a bland smiling face which masked one of the most vicious personalities in 'B' Division.

'I've been working steady and going straight home,' said Albert.

'Dutiful husband, eh?'

'Just that,' snapped Albert. 'Why, d'you want to make something of it?'

'Don't get excited, Tiny's only having his little joke,' said Ned. 'That's right, int it, Tiny?'

'I don't want any cracks about my marriage, that's all,' said Albert.

'Sure, we understand, kid.' Ned lit one cigarette off the butt end of another, mashed the stub in a littered tray and went on: 'We thought we'd give you a week or two to settle down, but now we got a job lined up for you, Albert. A real belter that'll put us all on Easy Street for years, see?'

Albert eyed him directly. There was a small pause, then he said: 'I'm sorry, Ned . . .'

The big fella's hand dropped on his shoulder, grinding down on to the bone structure. 'What the hell d'you mean, you're sorry?' he demanded.

Albert wrenched himself free. 'I'm not running with the gang any more, I'm going straight, that's all.'

Ned blew a long stream of smoke in his face. 'I just told you this is a belting job, kid,' he purred. 'But we need a good jelly man to pull it off right . . . and that means you.'

Albert stirred uncomfortably. Then he said flatly: 'I'm through with all that, Ned.'

'Yeh?' Purdy's hard face was drained of expression. 'You want to know what'll happen if you don't come in with us, kid? We'll have to rough you up, you know that.'

'I'll have to take my chance, then, Ned.'

There was a pause, then Purdy said easily: 'All right, you'll take a doing-up from us. In that case we got another idea.'

'I'm not interested.'

'You will be.' Purdy grinned evilly.

'I've told you . . .'

'You'll be interested all right. You see, we'll have to do up your kid, Albert.'

Albert Bright looked from Ned Purdy to the rest of the gang; a ring of faces belonging to men from whom he could expect very little of mercy; men to whom casual and mindless violence was part of the job.

Tiny Harker pinched his blubbery underlip between a thumb and forefinger. 'We don't like having to do up a kid, but you're sort of forcing us,' he said cosily.

Purdy leaned back in his chair. 'How is the little fella, then?' he asked. 'We heard he ain't quite . . . well, not . . .'

'Shut up!' grated Albert. He pushed the table from him, stood up and said harshly: 'All right. I'll do it. But just this one time. It's the last I ever do, see.'

Ned Purdy's face beamed false joviality. 'Sure, Albert, we don't want to ask too much of a pal who's spent the last few years in stir.'

Watching his face, Albert understood quite well that it would not be the last demand made on him. There'd be another job, then another . . . until, in the end, he stood again in the dock at Assizes or Quarter Sessions with the certainty of another long and agonising separation from the wife and son he loved.

But he had another thought: if the loot was big enough he could emigrate with Joyce and Tommy, start a new life in Australia or Canada . . . anywhere beyond the evil reach of Ned Purdy and the Violet Gang.

'What's the job then?' he asked.

'That's our boy,' said Purdy. 'It's right up your alley, Albert.'

'What's in it for me?'

Purdy chuckled. 'I can see we got you interested,' he said. 'It's at a sub-station on the main railway line going south. British Rail takings it is, running into thousands.'

'What, in a sub-station office?'

'Yeh, bloody marvellous. The stuff is locked in a safe there overnight, in transit. They keep it there just one night. Only cash. Documents and stuff like that stay at the main-line terminus. They don't concern us at all. It's the loot we want, the ready. Only it's in this strong safe.'

'How strong?'

'It's a big safe, if that's what you mean.'

'I just wanted an idea of its size and strength, so's I'll know what to do. What about security?'

'Only the station-master. We'll fix him.'

'How?'

'No undue violence, kid,' answered Ned smoothly. 'You don't need to worry about that. We just tie him up and maybe stuff a gag in his mouth, that's all.'

'All right, Ned. When?'

'Tonight,' Purdy answered. 'It's all laid on.'

II

But there was a factor Ned Purdy hadn't taken into account—the effect of his blackmail on Albert Bright's relationship with his young wife, and in a very special way, with his son.

Since his release from prison Albert had stayed home every night, except when he had a long-distance haul. And tonight he was off duty, though for convenience his truck was parked on waste land opposite the small semi-detached house in which they lived—and he knew that Joyce would think it strange if he went out after their evening meal. But he had to do it.

All through dinner he had been oddly preoccupied and Joyce had not failed to notice this. But she said nothing. Then, when she was about to clear the table,

Albert said awkwardly: 'I just want to pop out for an hour, love.'

She half-turned with plates in her hand. 'Why, where are you going, Albert?'

He moved uneasily. 'Oh, I ran into a fella I used to know and he asked me if I'd have a pint with him,' lied Albert. He avoided meeting her eyes.

The sense of anxiety began to grow within her.

'What fella d'you mean?' she asked.

He shrugged. 'Bill Phillips,' he said.

'I've never yeard you mention him before, Albert.'

'Well, I haven't seen him for a heck of a time. What's it matter, any road?'

'Nothing,' Joyce said. 'Only . . .'

'Only *what*?' There was a hard edge to his voice, a voice usually quiet and affectionate. 'Why the hell shouldn't I go out for a pint?' he went on. Even in his own ears his tone sounded savage. He had never spoken to Joyce like that before and hadn't even meant to. He knew his nerves were playing him up. 'I'm sorry,' he muttered. 'I didn't want to shout at you.'

Joyce put the plates down and came close to him. She touched his hand, but still he didn't look at her—couldn't.

'Is . . . is everything all right, Albert?' she asked steadily.

'Yeh, sure . . . not to worry,' he said. Abruptly, he picked up his raincoat and went out. In his mounting anxiety he did not even speak to the Mongol son he loved and whose idol he was.

Tommy was already in bed, wondering why his father hadn't come upstairs to play with him and say good night. When he heard the door bang shut the little boy went to the window and watched his father leave the house and start walking across the space to the parked lorry.

Tommy ran down the stairs in a panic. His mother was in the kitchen and didn't see him. In another moment the boy had slipped out of the house and was running across the space. The lorry was already starting to move. There was a spare wheel on the back—and as the vehicle began to go through its gears Tommy Bright was wedged in the wheel . . .

Albert had arranged to pick up the gang in the dark mouth of a cobbled alleyway off Scotland Road. There were four of them including Ned Purdy, and they all clambered in without seeing the tiny figure clinging to the spare wheel behind.

'What about the station-master?' Albert asked as he drove off again.

Charley Dilkes, a scrawny tearaway with ratty blond hair, grinned. 'These'll fix him,' he said.

Ned Purdy eyed the brass knuckles the other had fitted over his right hand. 'Take them things off,' he ordered. 'We don't need no violence to tie up one fella.'

'I could put him out like a light, boss.'

'Sure you could, Charley boy. Happen *right* out, and then we have the Jacks really on our collar. Whaddyer want—ten years?'

Dilkes's jaw sagged.

'I thought that'd shake yer,' grinned Purdy. 'Now, listen, you nit—we'll fix the station-master without doing him up, see.'

'All right.'

'I said to take them things off, didn't I?'

Dilkes slid the brass off his hand. Ned Purdy took the knuckledusters from him and rammed them in a pocket. 'That's better,' he said. 'This way we don't have no trouble.'

Albert Bright drove on without words. Finally, he parked the lorry under the dark overhang of some trees a short distance from the sub-station and they all got out and started walking. They crossed a wooden foot-bridge in single file and closed in on the silent station like flitting shadows.

They had been gone only a few moments when Tommy Bright climbed down from the rear wheel and tripped unsteadily after them . . .

III

It was 12.29 a.m. when the alarm came in to the Information Room at Police Headquarters. Then the cool, unhurried voice of the girl radio announcer calling the Z-car squads.

Information to Z-cars. Gang of men, believed to be five in number, wearing masks or similar disguises, broke into British Rail sub-station 12.21 a.m. Understood to have stolen £7,600 from safe . . .

Alderson, the desk sergeant, said: 'Joe Gillibrand, the station-master—they tied him up and gagged him, but he managed to struggle partly free, enough to use the phone only a matter of minutes after they left.'

'No special guard mounted on that safe, then?' I said.

Alderson shook his head. 'No, just the station-master, Bill. The authorities reckon the takings are secure enough in that transit safe. Only railway people are supposed to know about the arrangement, anyway.'

'The gang must have pretty good information,' I grunted.

'Must have had.'

'They could have an inside contact,' I said. 'On the

other hand, they could have formed a shrewd idea of the situation by keeping tabs on the place over a period.'

'That's true.'

'This station-master, Joe Gillibrand—how far away does he live?'

'The house is nearby, only a matter of some yards. But he stays up when there's cash being left in the office safe. I reckon there'd be a light showing from the office it was in.'

'Not that that'd matter if the gang had already cased the place,' I said. 'I mean they'd go right in, anyway. But the real point is that all these villains had to do was overpower Gillibrand, tie him up and gag him and then the way would be clear.'

'That's it all right,' assented Alderson.

A Z-car crew came in just then for a supper break, but they didn't get it. They went right out again, and I rode with them. The safe door had been blown almost completely off its hinges. Inside, it was as barren as a conman's heart while he fleeces the old widow woman of her savings.

'D'you happen to know which way the gang went?' I asked Gillibrand.

'They didn't make off right away,' the station-master said. 'They lost a bit of time distributing the money among themselves. Oh, a right good time them fellas was having! Laughing and joking and cracking on about what they was going to do with all that cash and . . .'

'Yes,' I said a trifle testily, 'but where did they go?'

'I'm coming to that, Mr. Prendergast,' said the station-master ponderously. 'They'd slammed the office door shut and left me tied up. What they didn't realise was that I'd already managed to loosen the cords round my wrists, and just after they left I got my hands free. Even now they can't have been gone long.'

'Yes,' I said, 'but which way?'

'They crossed the footbridge,' Gillibrand replied. He scratched his chin. 'Wait a tick—I heard them saying something about having a lorry parked beyond the bend, over on't other side. That'd mean crossing the permanent way on both trips and they'll need to go slow and careful like because there's a live electric rail running down the middle.'

That seemed to give us at least a chance of catching up with them. Bert Rawlings and I went fast over the footbridge and turned right at the bottom of the steps. It was almost pitch-dark and a thin drizzle had started. You couldn't see more than a very short distance ahead. But, suddenly, Bert stopped.

'I can just hear something, Sarge,' he whispered. 'Down there—they must be crossing the tracks.'

'They must have stopped for some reason or they'd have been over the permanent way before now,' Jock Ewing said.

'Happen they weren't sure of the way back in this darkness,' said Bert.

'It doesn't matter,' I snapped. 'Let's get after them.'

We broke into a run. Suddenly, the moon sailed free of a cloudbank. When we neared the big bend, Bert stopped in mid-stride, clutching at me.

'For God's sake, there's a kid wandering on the line,' he gasped.

I thumbed the button of a big hand torch and the powerful beam speared into the dimness. lighting up the white face of a boy about four years old. I started to shout out to him, telling him not to move—but it was too late. There was a small white flash and a sobbing cry.

'Christ . . . he's on the live rail,' Bert said.

He turned and raced back to the car. When he returned he was carrying a rubber coat and a pair of rubber gloves.

He went down the embankment in a single leap, fell on his hands and knees, picked himself up and went out towards the rails.

Then he spread the coat, reached down and hauled the boy on to it, handing him up to me. 'It's all right, he's not dead, just burned,' Bert said in his stolid way. 'But we'd best get him to hospital right away.'

'Yes,' I said. 'Incidentally, you just saved his life.'

'Well, I couldn't leave him there, could I?'

'You might have copped it yourself—one false move in the dark,' I rejoined. 'Nice work, Bert.'

'Oh, I . . .' Bert stopped.

We turned together. In the far distance, on the other side of the permanent way, an engine rumbled into life. Then the sound faded and was gone.

'That'll be the gang making their getaway,' I said.

'Aye, and our car on the side of those damned tracks,' snorted Bert.

It was pointless to follow. While Bert took the burned boy to hospital, I had a multiple call put out for the parents of any missing child. Then the Z Victor Two arrived and I went in it to the hospital. I had seen that the boy was a Mongol. There seemed little likelihood of his being able to tell us anything that would yield a clue, but I had a feeling that something might happen that night—and if it did I wanted to be on hand.

The wait wasn't long. Around two-thirty in the morning Albert Bright walked into the hospital. His face was lined and haggard with anxiety. Behind him was his young wife.

'Hello, Albert,' I said.

He blinked rapidly. 'What're you doing here, then, Mr. P.?' he faltered.

'I could ask you that question,' I said.

He swallowed convulsively, then went on in a rush:

'Our little lad's gone missing. I . . . we wondered if he'd met with some accident like and couldn't tell what happened. He . . . he don't always speak too well.'

'I know, Albert.'

'You know that . . . how?'

'Your son is here, in the hospital. He's in bed. The doctor's been with him.'

Joyce Bright was struggling for words, but her husband got them out first. 'What's the matter then, for God's sake is Tommy hurt?'

'Not badly.'

'He must've wandered out of the house,' said Albert. 'Joyce didn't, I mean we didn't know. What's happened? Some bloody car . . .'

I put a hand on his arm. 'No, it wasn't that.' I looked levelly at him as I added: 'He was crossing the main railway line at the big bend near the sub-station when he touched a live rail . . .'

'Oh, dear God!' whispered Joyce Bright.

'But he's all right,' I went on. 'He's burned, but not seriously, as it happens. He's going to be all right, the doctor says.'

Albert circled an arm round his trembling wife and stood there without words but with an odd expression on his face.

'You don't happen to know how he could possibly have come to be on the permanent way, so far from his home and at that time of night, do you, Albert?'

I could see him pulling himself together. 'No, it's a right mystery, Mr. P. I can't think how it come about.'

'Was the little boy in bed when you went out tonight?' I asked.

His eyes flickered. 'I didn't say I went out,' he said.

'So you didn't, I wasn't thinking. Did you, though?'

'I went out for a pint with a fella I used to know. What's it matter?'

'*Was* Tommy in bed at that time?'

'Well, yeh, he was.'

'You're a lorry driver now, aren't you?'

'What about it?'

'I just wondered if you kept the vehicle near your home some nights, like when you've finished a long haul or something like that.'

He stood there, his face schooled to show nothing. But his wife glanced nervously at him. I wondered.

But I didn't press the point. Instead, I said deliberately: 'A gang of masked men got away with seven thousand six hundred pounds from the safe at the railway sub-station. Somebody jellied the safe, Albert—somebody with knowledge. Only an expert jelly man could have done it so efficiently and rapidly.'

He ran a tongue across dry lips, but his voice was defiant. 'Yeh? Well, I'm on the straight, Mr. P. I only come out a few days ago; well, a week or so. Would I stick my neck out like that?'

'He's really been trying to go straight, Mr. Prendergast,' said Joyce.

'I believe you, Mrs. Bright . . .' I broke off as the night sister came up. She said they could see the injured boy.

'You go in first, Mrs. Bright,' I said. 'I just want to clear up a point with Albert.'

She hesitated. 'Go on, love, I'll join you in a minute,' Albert said. He turned back to me and went on: 'It's right what she told you. I been trying to go straight.'

'You used to go around with Ned Purdy's Violet Gang, didn't you?'

'Yeh, but I keep telling you . . .'

'You don't need to, Albert. I don't believe you would get out of line—not this time and not willingly. But there might have been some, shall we say, persuasion?'

'I got nothing to tell you, Mr. P.,' Albert said woodenly.

'Your little lad worships you, doesn't he?' I said.

He didn't answer. I thought of the little boy being so far from home. There could be only one reason for his being there and only one way he could possibly have got there . . . unseen on the lorry his father was driving. I knew it, but I knew no less surely that I had no way of proving it or proving Albert Bright's complicity in the crime at the railway station.

But perhaps there *was* a way. I didn't want to take it, but I heard myself saying slowly: 'A police officer saved your boy's life, Albert. He spread a rubber coat over the track and crawled out and lifted Tommy on to it. That's why he's still alive . . . and for no other reason.'

For a long moment he stood there staring at me, his thin face working. Then he said wonderingly: 'A copper. . . . a copper did *that*?'

'Yes. He risked his own life.'

Albert Bright stood erect. 'Can I see him, please?' he asked.

'He's just coming into the room,' I replied.

Albert Bright went up to him and said, very slowly and in a voice that was only just audible: 'You did that for my kid? You dragged him off a live rail and saved his life?'

'It's all right,' answered Bert. 'Any fella would've done the same thing.'

'A copper . . .' Albert seemed to be saying the hated word to himself.

'Even coppers are human beings, Albert,' I said. 'You've never stood in the dock at the Old Bailey, have you?'

'No and I don't want to, neither,' he said. 'Why?'

'Oh, there's a sign in the Old Bailey. It's sort of a police motto. It says *Defend and protect the children of the poor.* We try to do that as well as knocking off villains, Albert.'

He turned to face me fully and said in a clear, even voice: 'I reckon one good turn deserves another, Mr. P. I jellied that safe all right . . . it was me and the Violet Gang . . .'

IV

The long night had almost gone and a grey dawn was moving over the sleeping city. Bert Rawlings was driving me home. We were nearly there and still I hadn't spoken.

'What's to do, Bill?' asked Bert quietly.

'I suppose I was just thinking.'

'I imagined you'd be pleased, getting Albert Bright to confess like that. If you hadn't told him about me saving his little lad he probably wouldn't have done.'

'I know, that's what was on my mind.'

'What's wrong, then?'

I got out of the car, leaned in the window and said: 'Albert's not a real villain like Ned Purdy, not at heart. I almost wish I hadn't told him.'

'You *had* to make him confess,' said Bert soberly. 'You *had* to do it. That's police work . . .'

'Yes,' I answered. 'Good night, Bert.'

5

The Killer

Early one evening I was reading the crime sheet, which was no way to pass the time because it was calculated to strike alarm and despondency in the bosom of any conscientious policeman.

Covering a period of one month, it listed nine cases of breaking and entering at jewellers' shops in as many different sections of the city, representing a total loss to the owners of not less than £10,000.

Detective Inspector Sam Goodyard came into the room, tossed his hat on a side table and said: 'A bit of nice light reading, eh, Bill?'

'I doubt if the Super will endorse that description,' I grunted.

'He doesn't,' answered Sam drily. 'In point of fact, he's what's known as hopping mad. Nine major cases and not a single one solved. And now the newspapers are baying at our heels. Harsh words from the Chief Constable, demands for action in the Watch Committee . . . why be a copper?'

'We'll settle this lot in the end, Sam,' I said stolidly.

'Aye, happen we will—if we're not demoted and put back to pounding a beat in the meantime,' rejoined the D.I. lugubriously.

'Sooner or later Brad Holder's going to make just one slip,' I argued.

'The question is—can we afford to wait?'

'We have to, Sam. I don't mean we all sit around on our backsides waiting. Every man on the strength has been briefed to keep eyes and ears open for the smallest sign, either from Holder himself or Eddie Rostron. By this time they'll be starting to think they can't put a foot wrong—and that's usually the point at which they're liable to make the slip.'

'You're still positive in your own mind that they're behind all this, aren't you?'

'I've never been more certain of anything, Sam.'

'The Super's beginning to have doubts on that score,' Goodyard announced. 'He wonders if you're really looking in the right direction.'

'Every scrap of information I've been able to uncover points to Brad,' I said. 'All right, so he's a bookmaker running a legitimate business. But that's by day and it's a cover for the way he really piles up money. The Bentley he's just bought didn't come out of the proceeds of back-street bookeying—and I hear he's negotiating for a luxury flat out at Sefton Park.'

'That doesn't prove anything, Bill, you know that.'

'All right, I know it. But there are others factors, not least the sure knowledge that Brad Holder is the leader of the best-organised gang we've had to deal with in a decade.'

'That's putting two and two together from scraps of information and your well-known intuition, Bill . . . it's not knowledge.'

'Not in the sense that it's admissible as evidence in a court of law, but, dammit, we have to start somewhere. I'm starting on the virtual certainty that Brad Holder, with Eddie Rostron as his chief leg-man, are the brains behind the break-ins.'

A faint smile moved briefly on the D.I.'s rugged face.

'You don't have to convince me, Bill,' he rejoined. 'But you *do* have to convince both the Chief and the Super, and they're beginning to wonder if you're not barking up the wrong tree.'

'They're not taking me off this line of investigation, are they?' I asked.

'Not yet, no. But, by God, you'll have to produce results pretty soon.' Goodyard lit a cigarette, waved the match up and down until the small flame died and added: 'The Super wants to know where the stuff is fenced—or rather, who's fencing it. I told him we've checked on every known receiver without result.'

'Sure,' I said sardonically. 'They're all clean . . . because, unless I'm utterly and completely wrong, Brad Holder is not only the organiser of the robberies but the fence as well. Three times in the last month he's been away from his office for two consecutive days, leaving Eddie Rostron to run the place. As to where he's been, your guess is as good as mine.'

'London, you mean?'

'Amsterdam, perhaps.'

'If he's booked flights from Speke or Ringway airports we could check that.'

'I've already done that, Sam. No bookings. But he wouldn't risk booking there in case he was spotted. Nothing to stop him going to London, though, and booking at Heathrow under another name and with a false passport.'

'Customs—how about Customs?'

'I agree that's a risk, but it's being done every day and not always detected. Mind you, he could just drive to the Smoke and dispose of the stuff to a contact there.'

'We'd better put a twenty-four-hour watch on his apartment, then, and stop him on any pretext the next time he sets out in his posh Bentley.'

'I've arranged that, Sam. But for the past week he's made no such move. It's my guess he's beginning to get wary of us.'

'Charming,' said Goodyard. 'That leaves us precisely nowhere.'

'Not quite. I'm personally keeping an eye on two villains who I know are in with him.'

'Who?'

'Ben Watchmaker and Joey Shanks.'

'Watchmaker,' mused the D.I. 'A double-dyed villain, the one they call Big Ben.'

'Yes, an inevitable nickname. I've more than a hope I may be able to catch them out.'

'When?' asked Goodyard sombrely.

I picked up my hat, got as far as the door and turned back. 'Tonight,' I said and left before Sam could fire any more questions at me.

In fact, all I had to go on was a tiny scrap of information obtained in a back-street pub not far from the Pierhead. But it was interesting information, maybe even better than if it had come from an informer. I had gone into the pub through the side entrance and had instantly spotted Big Ben and Joey sitting at a corner table drinking black-and-tans. I stood on the threshold, listening. They had no notion that I was there and I was able to catch fragments of their conversation.

One in particular held my attention. Big Ben Watchmaker was talking in a rumbling undertone. 'Everything's fixed, then,' he said. 'Eleven on the dot at Jamieson's place in Lower Croft Street. Here's to it . . .'

He raised the pint to his lips with a laugh and I left immediately. It was true, of course, that eleven on the dot could mean tomorrow night or some other night, but I didn't think so. The small note of urgency in Big Ben's heavy voice suggested that it was to be later tonight.

I resolved to handle this one alone. If they didn't show up I had merely guessed the wrong night and would try again. But if I was right . . . well, I could call the Z-cars on the 'blower' or call assistance on my handset.

I parked my own car in a pool of dark and walked into Lower Croft Street. The small jewellery shop belonging to the Exors of J. H. Jamieson was about threequarters of the way down on my right. I walked slowly, treading on the balls of my feet. A sudden wind arose, stirring torn paper in the gutter. There was no other sound or movement; the entire street was deserted at this hour.

Then, suddenly, I saw them—two figures moving from the opposite end of the street. They halted outside the shop. I flattened myself in another doorway and called Headquarters on the miniature radio handset.

There was a pause. Then the girl announcer's voice came back: 'Z Victor One and Z Victor Two being ordered to proceed to Lower Croft Street at once . . . area will be cordoned, both ends of the street . . . over and out.'

I could have waited for the cars, but I don't like hanging back. I went fast along the pavement. The door of the shop was ajar. I stepped inside. They were ramming rings, watches and bracelets into a black sack.

I had made no sound, but some sixth sense must have warned Big Ben. He wheeled, his hand making a darting movement and coming up and out with a woven-leather blackjack. But I had held the welterweight boxing championship of the Liverpool City Police . . . and the fist which connected with Big Ben's craggy jaw seemed to have lost little of its power. The impact was hard and snapping. Big Ben rocked back on his heels, then swayed forward in time to take a short-arm jab to the solar plexus. A sound like air escaping from a punctured balloon wheezed distressedly from him and he went down on his hands and knees.

Joey Shanks shrilled: 'It's a fair cop, Mr. P. I'll come quiet.'

There was a rush of feet and the shop was suddenly full of uniformed men. Ten minutes later Big Ben and Joey were in the cells at Police Headquarters and Sam Goodyard was telling me, quite properly, that I was a member of a team, not a lone-wolf private detective solving crimes on his own.

'I agree, Sam,' I said. 'But I just wanted to be sure I hadn't made a false deduction. Anyway, I called Headquarters.'

'Yes—and went in alone. Those hooks might have done you up.' A grin crinkled the ends of his mouth. 'Not that you seem to have been incapable of handling the situation,' he remarked drily. 'You certainly gave Big Ben something to ponder over in the silent watches of the night.'

The phone rang. It was the Chief. The D.I. took the call. When he put the receiver back he said: 'The old man's pleased, but says he'll be more pleased when you get Big Ben and Joey to cough the rest . . . well, he didn't use that word, but you know what he means.'

'Yes,' I said slowly, 'but I'm betting that neither Big Ben nor Joey will grass on Brad Holder.'

'Start the chatting,' said Goodyard tersely.

It lasted far into the night. If you keep it up long enough, men begin to trip up. They lose track of the lies they have told you and, at some point or other, betray themselves. But this was different. Big Ben just sat there smoking cigarettes and incessantly repeating: 'I got nothin' to say, Mr. P. Nothin' at all, see?'

The weak link could have been Joey Shanks, but his very cowardice kept his mouth shut. I used the well-tested tactic of questioning them separately, but it was no use. Joey was frightened all right—but he was more frightened of gang vengeance than the prospect of yet another stretch in Walton.

In the end I had to admit defeat. They were brought before the magistrates' court, committed for trial and sentenced to three years, still maintaining that they had pulled the job on their own. All I had succeeded in doing was to catch a couple of small fish; the big sharks were still in the swim.

But now a seemingly baffling thing happened. The break-ins ceased—as suddenly as though a tap had been turned off.

'The convictions must have thrown a scare into Brad and Eddie,' mused the D.I. He eyed me levelly and added: 'What do you think?'

'The same as you, Sam—that they're just taking a rest. We haven't heard the last of them.'

'You reckon they'll start the break-in lark again when things have blown over?'

'Perhaps.'

'Or try something different?' suggested Goodyard sagely.

'I've been wondering about that,' I said.

Two nights later I dropped in at a pub off Lime Street, looking for information, anything which might point to Brad Holder. The public bar was jammed and the atmosphere was thick enough to carve up in solid chunks. I hadn't been there more than a few minutes when Holder thrust his way in. He was a heavily built man in his early forties with a small puckered scar just above the left temple and a roll of flesh overriding the collar of a forty-guinea suit cut several degrees too sharp. He saw me almost at once, but gave no sign of recognition. Instead, he turned abruptly and went out. I left my untasted drink and went after him.

When I reached the pavement he was already a short distance down the street, getting into his car. Two figures approached. Holder wound the driving window down, poked his head out and said something and they got into the car. Holder flicked his winking lights on, swung the car out from the kerb and drove down towards Lime Street—but not before I had identified the two men.

I went back to Headquarters. Sam Goodyard was on the point of going out, but the moment he saw me he said: 'You've got a bit of news, I can tell. Come through into the office.'

He closed the door and said: 'Well?'

'I was in a pub when Brad Holder came in. The moment he spotted me he went straight out. I followed and saw two men get in his car and drive off . . . they were Tod Dukes and Ginger Barton.'

The D.I.'s jaw stiffened. 'The worst strong-arm men in the manor,' he said. 'I don't like it, Bill.'

'I don't like it myself,' I answered. 'They've both been put down for common assault, grievous bodily harm and demanding money with menaces. It could be suggestive.'

'Yes,' said Goodyard slowly. 'If Holder's recruiting villians specialising in thumping we could be in for something unpleasant—but what?'

'I don't know—yet.'

Goodyard paced up and down the floor. 'I don't like waiting until some inoffensive citizen gets beaten up,' he said, 'we're supposed to prevent crime as well as arrest the criminals.'

'Well, it might have been a sort of chance meeting.'

'You don't believe that, do you?'

'Frankly, no, but we can't put even Dukes and Barton

down merely for riding in Brad Holder's car.'

'Look, did they see you?'

'Holder spotted me in the pub, but I'm certain he didn't see me after that, nor the others. I didn't move out of the doorway more than a foot or two.'

'That helps,' Sam reflected. 'I mean it helps because Holder doesn't know you saw him with these hooks. I'll have a message put out to all the cars. They might run into something.'

I sighed. 'It's the old waiting game, Sam, but I don't see what else we can do.'

The wait wasn't long, though. No more than twenty-four hours. Z Victor One was on patrol, turning off the Prescot Road into Back Bowling Street when Jock Ewing said: 'Hold it, Bert—there's a man lying in the gutter.'

'Probably a drunk,' answered Rawlings as he brought the car to a halt.

The man was lying on his side with his right arm at an odd angle. He reeked of whisky, but he wasn't drunk, as a test showed later. Whisky must have been poured on him. He had a broken arm and several of his front teeth were smashed.

Jock signalled Headquarters to send an ambulance and said: 'I know this fella. It's Fred Colley—he runs a bit of a club round here. Tatty strip shows and gambling.'

Bert, who had put a rolled-up coat under the injured man's head, said: 'Well, he certainly stinks of booze.'

Colley put a hand to his bloodied mouth and mumbled: 'Took a drop too much . . . must've tripped up . . . hit myself on the edge of the kerb . . .'

'What, an' broke your arm as well?' Bert stared down at him. 'What were you doing out of your club at this time, any road?' he demanded.

'Stepped out for a breather . . . the night air must've knocked me out . . .' Colley winced.

Then the ambulance came. Jock unhooked the two-way radio telephone and got through to Headquarters. The message was brought to the detective's room immediately.

Sam Goodyard and I read it together. 'A pound to a penny he was beaten up,' Sam commented.

'He's not lodged a complaint, Sam.'

'No, according to Ewing and Rawlings, he claims he fell in the gutter, but I don't believe a word of it. Get round to the casualty ward and see if you can do anything with him.'

'All right,' I said.

It was no use, though. All I could get out Fred Colley was a stolid reiteration of the tale he had told the Z-car team.

'You're lying,' I said.

'Why would I do that?' he muttered.

'Reprisals,' I said. 'The fear of something even worse than what you've already had. You've been beaten up and you're scared to tell me. That's it, isn't it?'

'I got nothing to say,' he answered shakily.

I made one more try. 'If you'll confide in us we'll arrange police protection, Mr. Colley . . .'

His hurt mouth made a small, wry twist. Then he turned his face from me.

I didn't go back to Headquarters immediately. Instead, I drove to Brad Holder's bookmaking office. Eddie Rostron was behind the counter, a dark-haired fellow pushing thirty with a sensual face and a hearty manner as false as a crooked used-car salesman's.

'Why, hello there, Mr. Prendergast,' he said. 'Having a little flutter, like?'

'Where's the boss?' I asked curtly.

'In the back. I'll tell him you're here, shall I?'

'Don't bother,' I said. I lifted the counter flap and went into the rear room.

Brad Holder was totting up figures on long slips of paper. He took an eight-inch cigar from his mouth and said: 'Well, this is a surprise. Nothing the matter, is there?'

'I thought perhaps you could tell me that, Holder.'

'Who, me? I don't get mixed up in your work, Mr. Prendergast.'

'That's fine. Just keep it that way, then.'

He stood up, his eyes glinting. Then he banished the look from them and went on affably: 'I'm afraid I don't know what you're talking about. I run a legitimate business.'

'And make enough to live like a pop singer at the top of the charts, eh?'

He spread both hands in a wide gesture. 'Why not? Business is good.'

'Even the business in a back-street dump like this?'

He held the cigar at an angle, peering along it in a studied gesture of insolence. Then he looked back at me and said: 'If you've just come here to be bloody rude you can get lost, copper.'

'A club owner named Fred Colley was badly beaten up earlier tonight,' I said.

He blew a stream of blue smoke, fanned it away with his free hand and said: 'Never heard of him. Too bad if he got done over, though.'

'Happen it'll be too bad for whoever had it done.'

'And what's that supposed to mean?'

'Just something you might like to ponder,' I said and left.

I wasn't sure whether it was a wise move seeing Holder, except that it might save others from being beaten up—or betray Holder into some course of action which would give a clue. But I knew I had no proof and he knew it, too. The thing that preoccupied me was why Colley had been attacked. It was possible that he had welshed on a big credit bet and been given the traditional treatment, but I had a feeling there was more to it than that.

A week passed. Nobody else was found beaten up in the gutter and no complaints of violence to the person reached us. But I could not rid my mind of the thought that what had happened to Colley was no isolated attack, that, in fact, it could be part of a pattern.

'I've got the same feeling, Bill,' said Sam Goodyard. 'But if nobody's being done up we could both be wrong.'

'Suppose we make a systematic round of the pubs and clubs to see if we can drop on something?'

'It might help, yes,' replied the D.I. meditatively. 'What's your exact plan?'

'Myself and a couple of detective constables—Blake and Manning. So far as the pubs are concerned we can go in and out how we like, but for the clubs it'll be necessary to sign the membership book. Nothing to stop us, though.'

'Nothing,' Sam agreed. 'All right, do it and we'll see what turns up.'

For ten days nothing did. Then we started to hear things. They began with the unexplained absence of Tom Brewster and George Cohen, both of whom ran clubs. Since previously they had always been seen mingling with the members, their disappearance was puzzling and questions were asked. Cohen, who owned the Silver Star Club in the city, employed a manager named Tim Finney.

'Hey, where's George these last few nights?' someone demanded.

'Got a touch of the flu, be back in a day or two,' replied Finney.

'He looked well enough t'last time I saw him,' the customer said.

'Well, it hit him sudden like, all of a heap—you know,' Finney answered. There was a slightly evasive quality in his voice. Then he went into the office.

That left me standing close to the man who had questioned him. I said tentatively: 'Funny about George, eh?'

The other eyed me for a moment, and then said: 'You're a Jack, aren't you?'

'Well?'

'Nothing, only don't get the idea nobody here has rumbled you.'

'I can visit clubs, but I've never tried to pretend I wasn't in the C.I.D.,' I said. 'Or, putting it another way, I'm not denying it if asked. It's still odd about George Cohen.'

'Yeh, it's funny all right.' He seemed to be on the point of saying something, then apparently thought better of it and started to move away. I shot out a hand and grabbed his arm.

'You have the look of a man with a bit of worry on his mind,' I said.

I thought he was about to wrench himself away, but instead he suddenly nodded.

'Come and have a drink with me, Mr. . . .?' I said.

'Higgins, Sid Higgins.' He glanced swiftly round the smoke-filled room. If he was looking for Ginger and Tod there was no sign of them.

'If you don't want to talk here there's a boozer round the corner and it's not yet closing time,' I said.

'It might be better,' he rejoined.

The lounge bar of the pub was busy but not jammed.

I navigated a way to the table in a far corner and bought two pints of mixed.

'Now, what's worrying you, Mr. Higgins?' I asked quietly.

He sank about half his drink, passed the back of a hand over his mouth and said: 'I think George Cohen has been done up, that's what.'

'Any reason for that thought?'

He didn't reply for a moment. Then he lit a cigarette, leaned a little forward and said: 'There's sort of a funny atmosphere in the clubs just at present. I go into at least half a dozen—I'm a great club man—and I can tell.'

'What kind of atmosphere?'

'I can't just put a word to it, but it's sort of . . .'

'Like fear?'

He nodded. 'That's about it. I don't so much mean among the members but the fellas who run the places.'

'So I've noticed. I've been making the rounds of the clubs. There's something wrong. It's not easy to get information, though. As a manner of fact, you're the first man I've met who was willing to talk.'

He laughed shortly. 'Well, I wouldn't say I've given you much information. It's just an impression I get. But one thing I do know—George Cohen was as right as a trivet a few nights ago, never even hinted at having so much as a bad cold. And now he's suddenly out of sight.'

'What makes you think he might have been done up, Mr. Higgins?'

This time he let his gaze swivel round the men in the bar. I had never seen any of them before. He seemed to be reassured.

'Two fellas come in t'club a few nights ago,' Higgins said. 'Two fellas I've seen lately in other clubs and every time they come in there's kind of a funny atmosphere, like the club bosses suddenly got the wind up.'

'Two fellas,' I said evenly, 'two fellas like Tod Dukes and Ginger Barton?'

He started nervously and again his eyes ranged round the room. 'They're not here,' I said. 'It's all right, you're safe.'

'Look, I don't want to get in wrong with fellas like them two,' he muttered.

'If you want to go, it's all right, Mr. Higgins,' I replied. 'You've told me enough to be going on with.'

He finished his pint and stood up. 'I wouldn't have gone this far except for one thing,' he said.

'Oh, what's that?'

'George Cohen married my sister—and I can see she's half out of her mind with fright!'

He turned and went straight out of the bar. I sat on there for a few minutes, then I got my own car and went to see George Cohen. He didn't live over the club but had a detached house in the Knotty Ash district. His wife answered the doorbell. She was fortyish, a rinsed blonde putting on a little weight.

When she saw me a small choked cry came from her and she tried to shut the door. I put one of my big feet in it and said: 'It's all right—I'm a police officer. Prendergast, detective sergeant, C.I.D.'

'Oh!' she whispered.

'May I step inside, Mrs. Cohen?'

She hesitated, then held the door open. I followed her halfway down the hall. Then she stopped and said in a low voice. 'George'll half kill me letting a policeman into the house, only . . .'

'Only what, Mrs. Cohen?'

A violent trembling possessed her. 'I'm terrified. . . oh, my God, I'm nearly crazy with terror . . . it's got to stop . . .' Her voice scaled into near-hysteria.

There was a door further down the hall. From behind it a man's voice shouted: 'What's up? Who is it, Ruthie?'

I pushed the door wide open and went in. George Cohen was lying on a settee. He was wearing a dressing-gown and was unshaven. He couldn't shave on account of having a bandage round both sides of his face. His eyes looked clouded with lack of sleep. They were also clouded with something else . . . fear.

'Why, hello, Mr. Prendergast,' he said. 'What brings you here?'

'What the heck's happened to your face?' I asked.

'I had a bit of a bump in the car and cut myself—glass,' he said. '*You* know.'

'I'm not sure that I do, Mr. Cohen. Car badly damaged?' Even as I put the question I could see the sudden look in his eyes. Not so much fear now. This time it was apprehension. I went on: 'Mind if I see your car?'

'It . . . it's gone for repair . . .'

'Where?' I said roughly.

He put on a weak show of indignation. 'What the hell has it got to do with you, then?' he shouted. 'I don't have to . . .'

Ruth Cohen swung round on him. 'For God's sake, why don't you tell Mr. Prendergast what happened?' she begged. 'He's a police officer, a detective, he'll . . .'

George Cohen half rose from the settee. 'Shut up, will you?' he yelled. A spasm of pain took him and he sank back, gasping.

'Your back's hurt, too, Mr. Cohen,' I said levelly. 'What did they do—put the boot in your spine as well as cut your face?'

He lay there, breathing harshly. There was a panic glitter in his eyes. 'I got nothing to tell you,' he whispered.

'Who's your doctor?'

'It's Dr. Leroy Maurice,' said Ruth Cohen.

A look which was an amalgam of rage and fear ravaged his face. He began to yell at her, but I stopped him.

'I'm going to see your doctor, Mr. Cohen,' I said. 'Meanwhile, you'd best not lift a finger to your wife because if you do I'll give a story to the newspapers . . . and your name will be in it!'

He shivered. 'I'll not touch her,' he muttered. 'For heaven's sake, don't get my name in the papers over this—*please*!'

'It was Tod Dukes and Ginger Barton, wasn't it?' I asked.

'I got nothing to tell you, Mr. Prendergast. Leave me alone, will you?'

'Before I'm through you're going to *have* to tell me,' I said grimly. 'You and God knows how many more. 'What is it—extortion?'

He stared at me dumbly.

Dr. Maurice was professionally cautious. 'The patient had a badly cut face on the left side and substantial bruising in the lumbar region, both externally and to the bone structure,' he said.

'Did you form a conclusion that all this might have been the result of an attack?'

He shrugged. 'It could be,' he rejoined. 'In fact, that was my first impression—but Mr. Cohen insisted that he had been involved in an accident with his car.'

'In your opinion as a medical man, *were* his injuries consistent with his having been in a crash, doctor?'

'It's possible.'

'But you don't think so?'

'Frankly, I had some doubts. But in the circumstances, I felt obligated to accept the patient's word. I take it that you have formed a specific view of your own?'

‘I think a gang attacked him, slashed his face and then kicked him in the spine as he lay on the ground.’

‘I see. It’s rather horrible, isn’t it?’

‘Yes, very. The trouble is that so far I have no evidence and Cohen won’t talk because he is obviously an extremely frightened man.’

‘It’s not many years since the majority of criminals avoided violence as an act of policy,’ the doctor reflected.

‘We’re dealing with a different type of criminal these days, I’m afraid.’

He fingered his smoothly shaved chin. ‘I’m a humane man, Mr. Prendergast,’ he said. ‘On principle I am opposed to the return of either capital or corporal punishment, but I sometimes wonder if I’m right.’

By week’s end there were five more cases of managers or owners of pubs or clubs missing from their accustomed places. All of them had an interesting collection of cuts and bruises and two had broken bones. But no single one of them would admit to having been beaten up. The reign of terror was on.

‘The Chief says he wants action, Bill,’ the D.I. said.

‘There’s nothing *we’d* like better,’ I growled, ‘but wanting it and finding a way to get it are two very different things.’

‘Well, if *you* can’t induce one of ’em to talk nobody else can.’

‘The tribute is much appreciated, Sam, but just the same I feel that I may have slipped up somewhere.’

‘How?’

‘I don’t know—except that somewhere along the line there must have been an opening. Perhaps only the mere hint of an opening and I didn’t spot it.’

‘Keep on the case, Bill,’ said the D.I. ‘Something will turn up.’

But a few days later there seemed to be no case—for,

as suddenly as they had begun, the attacks ended. The wounded club owners were back on their premises and there were no more rumours of anybody else getting the treatment.

I was still going the rounds, when, one night, I called in at a dance hall in the Everton district. The place was jammed with teenagers dancing to a pop group whose amplified guitars made more din than a thirty-piece orchestra. It was a relief to wedge myself into the office and close the door on the noise.

'These groups do make a hell of a row, but the kids love it, and I give 'em what they pay for,' Frank Clewes said with a grin. He was a rangy fellow with a face like an amiable horse and was doing very nicely with the business, which he owned. He unlocked a cabinet and said over his shoulder: 'Will you have a drink?'

'Yes.'

'I've got some good Scotch,' Clewes said. He poured two and said: 'I take it you're here in the line of duty?'

'You take it correctly, Mr. Clewes. I've been making extensive inquiries into the reason why a number of club owners and similar characters have been nursing unexplained injuries.'

'Why come to me?'

'I haven't ruled out the possibility that the owner of a prosperous dance hall might find himself on the list.'

'I'm not sure I get you—what list?'

'That was just in a manner of speaking,' I said. 'Putting it bluntly, it seems to me that the men who have been injured were beaten up by a gang and for hard monetary reasons. It occurred to me that they were not likely to leave out other businesses known to be doing well.'

'Why should I be concerned, Mr. Prendergast?'

'Dance hall owners, like club managers and pub owners, are easier to get at—especially at night—than what we might call ordinary businessmen,' I said.

He didn't answer and after a moment I went on: 'Look, Mr. Clewes, if there *is* anything . . .'

He smiled, a fine wide smile. 'I haven't been threatened and I'm not likely to be,' he said.

'Oh, why?'

For a moment he seemed to hesitate, then he said evenly: 'There'll be no more attacks, Mr. Prendergast. We're making bloody sure of that.'

'How?'

The fine wide smile ebbed. 'Just leave it at that,' he said, 'and have another drink.'

'No thanks.' I picked my hat off his desk and said clearly: 'I've a message for you, Mr. Clewes—for you and any others with whom you may be associated. It's just this—leave police work to the police. It's what we're paid for and we're likely to do it better than anyone else.'

He made a small movement with his shoulders, not saying anything.

'Another thing—taking the law into your own hands can land you in a different kind of trouble.'

'Good night, Mr. Prendergast,' he said calmly.

I realised what was happening. The pubs and clubs and dance halls were organising their own bodyguards. This meant either that they had no confidence in the ability of the police to protect them—or, more probably, that they simply didn't relish being too closely involved with the law. I don't mean they were all dishonest men. What did occur to me was that even men who are honest in their business dealings sometimes have other things they would prefer to keep to themselves.

In the event, there was no vigilante violence. But commissionaries and other henchmen with bouncer written all over them suddenly appeared on the scene and the reign of terror ceased. Presumably, their mere presence was enough.

Then, one night when Z Victor One came in from a tour of duty, Jock Ewing said: 'Funny thing about those bodyguards, Sarge.'

'Oh, what's funny about them?'

'They've vanished.'

I stared. 'Vanished—where?'

'Och, I couldn't say, but they're not around any more.' Jock removed his peaked cap and rumpled his hair. 'All I know is that for the last two or three nights they haven't been there.'

'That's odd,' I reflected. 'You're quite sure?'

Bert Rawlings, who had joined us, interposed. 'It's right enough—not a sign of them.'

'Mind you,' said Jock, 'they mostly seemed to hang around about four or five places. Not every pub or club in the district. Some must've been sort of more vulnerable than others, though all the owners and managers put something in the kitty to pay these fellas.'

'And now, for no reason at all, they've been disbanded?'

'Happen there is a reason, Sarge. Brad Holder must've called the whole thing off. Scared, I mean.'

I couldn't understand it. By now I knew well enough that Holder had organised a highly profitable protection racket. The beatings-up had merely been warnings to men who wouldn't 'co-operate'. After that others, frightened of the ruthless violence, had met his demands. In other words, Holder was extorting regular money from a variety of sources, and it wouldn't be chickenfeed, either. That was why the bodyguards had been appointed, and the system must have worked. Then why had it suddenly been abandoned? It could just be that

Brad Holder had given up a profitable racket, but this I simply did not believe.

When I said as much to Sam Goodyard he agreed but added: 'If there's no more trouble, Bill, I don't quite see what we can do.'

'There's something behind this,' I answered. 'Something we haven't yet put a finger on. I'd like to keep on with the inquiries.'

'You're pretty well tied up just now with the docks stealing case, aren't you?'

'Yes, but it'll be complete in a day or two, and meantime I can move around the clubs at night.'

'Using up your free time, I suppose?' The D.I. grinned. 'Well, I can't stop you—but, remember, the force doesn't pay overtime for that.'

In the next few nights I sensed a new atmosphere in the clubs. Not so much fear as a kind of wooden resignation. It was difficult to analyse and did not seem to affect every place I visited, but five in particular—and I recalled what Jock Ewing had said about how the bouncers had mostly been noticed at four or five venues. I was positive that in some way Brad Holder and Eddie Rostron had succeeded in re-establishing their power—and this time without violence, for Dukes and Barton had left Liverpool for Manchester. But nothing I did yielded even the semblance of a clue.

It was a small incident, seemingly insignificant, which finally put me on the right track; though I could not know that it was to end in murder. I saw Eddie Rostron come up the steps from a small basement club near Rodney Street. He stopped against the lighted window of a shop and seemed to be examining something in his hand. I couldn't be sure what it was because he had his back towards me. Then he walked on.

I decided to follow.

It didn't take long. He finally reached a large, shabby-looking Victorian house made over into flats and let himself in. I waited a few moments, then strode into the vestibule. To the side of it there was a board covered with green baize and pinned to the board were a number of yellowed cards. One of them carried the legend: *E. Rostron, Flat Two.*

The door of the flat was ajar. I put the palm of my hand against it and pushed it wide open. Eddie Rostron was sitting at a gate-leg table counting a wad of notes. Opposite him was a slightly built young fellow with ash-blond hair and a smooth pale face which looked as if it would hardly ever need a shave.

Eddie Rostron had jumped up. 'What the hell d'you mean bustin' in here?' he yelled.

The blond young fellow said, in a soft, pleading tone: 'Don't get excited, Eddie . . .'

'You keep out of this, Stan,' snarled Eddie. 'I want to know what this Jack thinks he's up to, walking in on us like this.'

'Just a friendly call,' I said. I looked at the wad of notes, mentally counting about fifty pounds. 'Where did you get that?' I asked.

'That's my business.'

'Your business and mine might get mixed up in certain circumstances,' I said curtly.

'You can go and take a running jump in the Mersey . . .'

The slightly built boy looked at me out of gentle brown eyes. 'Are you a police officer?' he asked.

'Yes. Who are you?'

'Stan Collinson is my name. I live here. I mean we both live here, we share the flat, you know.'

'Don't talk to this Jack—leave him to me,' rasped Eddie.

'All right,' I said, 'let's talk. Where did you get that money?'

'What's it to you?'

'I saw you handling it when you came out of a club not more than fifteen minutes ago, a club near Rodney Street'

'So what?' He lit a cigarette and went on: 'All right, I won it if you want to know. I was playing blackjack in the club, see?'

'Oh, Eddie,' said Stan Collinson, 'you promised me you wouldn't go into places like that.'

'Oh, shut up!' Eddie turned back to me and said tightly. 'I won that dough ... try and prove anything different, Jack.'

'I might do that, Eddie,' I said. But I was no longer thinking of this particular wad of money, no matter how he had got it. I was thinking of Stan Collinson; specifically, of the almost feminine possessiveness in the way he had reproached Eddie.

It seemed to have nothing to do with any protection racket, but I could not rid my mind of it . . . and it was starting a train of entirely new thought.

By the time I got back to Headquarters I knew the answer. Goodyard listened without comment, then he said slowly: 'It fits. Your theory is that Rostron, still in league with Holder, is accusing his victims of making homosexual advances to him and then blackmailing them as the price of his silence.'

'I'm pretty sure of it, Sam, but if I hadn't seen Rostron with this young fellow he's living with I probably wouldn't even have suspected the new method Eddie and Brad Holder have dreamed up.'

'I never heard that any of these club fellows were queer, though,' said the D.I.

'Maybe they aren't, but they may have other things to hide, especially from their wives. Like a bird or two on the side. One thing I'm damned certain of—Holder and Rostron have chosen their victims carefully and the victims couldn't stand *any* kind of scandal, so they pay up.'

'Like I said, it fits,' Sam commented. 'But proof, we haven't a shred of proof.'

'If we don't let up we'll get it,' I said.

It took time and it involved careful and unobtrusive watching. A full month went by. I was starting to get impatient and decided to just walk boldly into the Brass Rail Club on the offchance of picking something up fast. The owner was a lantern-jawed fellow known as Sailor Hammond because he had once been a steward on the Atlantic run. He wasn't on view and I asked the club manager if I could have a word with him.

'He's in t'office with someone and he don't want to be disturbed,' the manager said. There was a worried look in his eyes.

I started across the fuggy room. The manager grabbed my arm. 'Don't go in, Mr. P,' he pleaded. 'Sailor'll go mad if I let you in.'

I knocked his hand away. 'You're not letting me in,' I said, 'I'm doing it myself.'

The door to the office was behind the bar. It was closed. I poked at it with an index finger. It opened fractionally—enough to see and hear.

Eddie Rostron was grinning evilly. 'Another fifty it is, Sailor—right here and now and no messing!'

Sailor Hammond was clenching and unclenching his massive fists. He could have felled Rostron with one blow.

'Don't try anything, Sailor,' taunted Eddie. 'Not unless you want it put around that you're queer. You been making propositions to me and if I don't get the fifty I came for I'm going to make plenty of trouble for you.'

'It's a filthy lie . . .'

'Don't talk crap, Sailor. It doesn't have to be true. The smear's enough. And imagine what your missus'll say ... you've had enough trouble already over the birds. You don't want her to think you're queer as well ...'

Sailor Hammond tilted a whisky bottle and drank about three inches of spirit. He slammed the bottle down on the desk, took money from a drawer and said thickly: 'Here's your dough, then. Now bloody well get out of here.'

'I'm on me way,' laughed Eddie. He picked up the money and pulled the door open. When he saw me practically every known emotion seemed to crowd into his face and vanish, except one—terror.

'You're under arrest, Rostron,' I said.

Suddenly the panic left him. 'Yeh—what for?' He half-turned and called: 'You just lent me fifty nicker, Sailor, just being an old pal, that's how it was—wasn't it?'

Sailor Hammond's craggy face was drained of expression. 'That's right, Eddie,' he said.

'You're still under arrest,' I snapped.

'Try and make it stick, Jack,' sneered Eddie. 'You can't make it stick, and you know it.'

'I overheard every word that passed between you two.'

'You got to have summat else,' said Eddie. 'What's the name the Jacks have for it? Co . . . I got it, corroborative evidence. And you ain't got any.'

There was a triumphant leer on his vicious face. I wiped it off for him. 'I'm knocking you off, Eddie,' I said, 'and then I'm going to chat Brad Holder . . . and what I'm thinking is that I'll get something this time.'

'You . . .' screamed Eddie Rostron.

It was still early in the night. Brad Holder would still be in his office—waiting for Eddie and the queer money.

I went there in the Z-car with Jock Ewing and Bert Rawlings.

Lights showed in the windows. I got out of the car and walked across the pavement. It was raining heavily, a gushing downpour which was sending the water down the sloping gutters like a river. There was an entry down one side of the office and I could see the impressive nose of Brad Holder's racing-green Bentley.

I had put out a hand to press the office doorbell when I noticed that the door itself wasn't locked, wasn't even on the latch. There was an aperture of about an inch.

I pushed the door inwards and stepped into the main room with Jock and Bert behind me. It was empty. We crossed the floor to the office at the rear. The door was wide open. There was no light inside. I reached a hand round the door, found the light switch and thumbed it down.

Brad Holder was lying on his back in the middle of the floor. The handle of a knife was jutting from his chest. Blood was pumping from him and his mouth was vivid with it.

'I'll call ambulance service,' said Jock.

I went down on one knee beside Brad Holder. His eyes met mine. Words came from him in a whisper: 'The kid who lives with Eddie . . . he come here and put the knife in me . . . I . . .' More blood moved on his mouth.

'That's enough for now,' I told him.

The ambulance crew arrived and took him to hospital. I followed in the Z-car. The surgeon came out and said: 'I've done what I could, but this man is going to die. He can't last an hour. He wants to speak to you . . . you'd better go in.'

I nodded. I had to put my ear close to Brad Holder's mouth to hear what he said. But it was enough. He coughed the whole facts of the racket.

'Why should the kid knife you?' I asked.

'I . . . don't know . . . I never even saw him before . . .' Holder made a small inarticulate sound. 'He said he was Eddie's friend . . . he said I was stealing him and . . .' Holder stared up at me. He fought for speech, but no more words came.

Another sound came from him, the last sound any man makes in this life. The doctor hurried in, but Brad Holder was dead.

I left at once and went to Eddie Rostron's flat. Stan Collinson was sitting in a chair watching television. I hadn't needed to knock because the door had been left half open.

'Is that you, Eddie, dear?' he called. 'Have they let you go, then?'

I walked on into the room. 'Why, Mr. Prendergast,' he cried in his soft voice. 'I didn't expect to see you!'

'I think you did.'

'Now why should you think such a thing?' he asked calmly.

'You are not obliged to say anything . . . I am going to charge you with the wilful murder of Bradley James Holder at about nine-fifteen tonight,' I said. 'It is my duty to warn you that anything you do say will be taken down and given in evidence.'

Stan Collinson stood up with a quick dainty movement. 'I'm sure I don't mind telling you what happened, Mr. Prendergast,' he said. 'I went to that office to see Eddie and Mr. Holder attacked me . . . in a certain way, you must understand. He resorted to violence and I only struck in self-defence.'

'With the knife you had conveniently brought with you?'

A gentle smile moved on his smooth face. 'Oh, no, you are quite wrong, Mr. Prendergast,' he said. 'Mr.

Holder had the knife and I managed to get it from him. It was so dreadful . . . the nature of his assault . . . what could I do but protect myself?'

'I think you're lying,' I said.

'I'm so sorry,' smiled Stan Collinson. 'But it doesn't really matter . . . it is what the jury think that will count, isn't it?'

Stan Collinson got seven years for manslaughter. The defence was admirably stated by his counsel: A mild young fellow warding off an obscene assault by a much older man know to be a gangster. It even had the ring of truth, but I knew it was false.

Eddie Rostron went down for five years for demandin money by menaces. When they were taken down to the cells I followed slowly after them.

'I hope you haven't come to gloat over us, Mr. Prendergast,' murmured Stan.

'You know better than that,' I said.

He touched Eddie's face with the tips of his fingers. 'I was right about what the jury would believe, wasn't I?' he said.

'Yes, you were right,' I replied harshly. 'But you lied, Stan, and Eddie backed you up by slandering the man he had worked with, a man who was dead and so couldn't answer back. But it wasn't manslaughter—it was murder. Deliberate, cold-blooded murder inspired by the special kind of soul-destroying jealousy which is worse than any wronged woman ever knows . . . the blind, tormented jealousy of the homosexual.'

Stan Collinson smiled his sweet, feminine smile. His soft brown eyes were gently reproachful.

'You thought Eddie was Brad Holder's sweetheart, so you killed him,' I went on. 'And the macabre joke is that they never were like that. They were just partners in crime, but you never knew that—you never even asked how Eddie got the money you both lived on.'

'Drop dead, copper,' whispered Eddie.

'They never were like that, Stan,' I repeated. 'But you and Eddie *are* . . . you're husband and wife.'

The slight, quiet boy who had knifed a man he didn't even know nodded eagerly. 'That's right, Mr. Prendergast. I realised you knew it that night when you came to our flat. But you can't do a thing about it, can you? Justice has been done.'

'It only *appears* to have been done,' I said. 'You should've been put down for life. As it is, you've got away with seven years, less remission.'

Neither of them spoke. I said harshly: 'I hope every minute of it is like an eternity.'

Stan Collinson smiled his gentle smile again . . . the quiet, effeminate man who had killed in cold blood and without even a reason other than his own twisted imagining.

'You don't understand us, Mr. Prendergast,' he said. 'You don't live in the same world. It won't seem long . . . and Eddie will be waiting. . . .'

6

The Big Dipper

I was just about to leave Headquarters on a windy autumn night when a dumpy little woman with an agitated manner came in through the main entrance and set about Sergeant Alderson without preamble.

A flood of semi-incoherencies poured over the luckless sergeant before he could ever inquire her name. I could have slipped out unnoticed by either of them.

Instead, I said in a loud ringing voice: *'Stop it!'*

The effect was magical. It was as if a chairman had arisen in the middle of a party political meeting and subdued the clamour of an unruly heckler. Well, they tell me my voice is fairly strong and I was using it at full volume.

The agitated woman bit her tongue and wheeled on me brandishing an umbrella. 'Who are you?' she stormed. 'What do you mean interrupting? You're not a policeman, you haven't got a uniform on.'

'He's C.I.D., ma'am, Detective Sergeant Prendergast,' explained Alderson desperately.

'Oh, is he?' The visitor didn't seem impressed. 'He made me bite my tongue,' she snapped.

'I'm sorry,' I said. 'What appears to be the trouble? Perhaps I can help.'

She eyed me up and down without any marked enthusiasm. 'A detective, eh? Well, you might do, I suppose. I've had me handbag pinched. Four pound ten and six gone out of me purse.'

'How and when did this sad event happen, ma'am?'

'I was waiting in Church Street for a bus, it must have been then. In fact, I'm sure it was. I felt somebody nudge into me while I was in t'queue.'

'Who?'

'Some young fella, I think.'

'Didn't you see him?'

'Well, not exactly see him, no. But I think it was a young chap. He was whistling one of them pop tunes, so he would be a young fella, wouldn't he?'

'Can you describe anything about him, Mrs. . . .?'

'Hancock is the name and I live at 6a Foley Street, Aigburth. Aye, you can write that down in your little book,' she said to Alderson. She turned back to me and went on: 'I've just said he was a young chap. That ought to be enough.'

'There are a lot of young men in this city, Mrs. Hancock,' I said patiently. 'We can't arrest them all, can we?'

She surveyed me with scarcely veiled disgust. 'I thought t'police were here to protect us,' she said coldly.

'You're right to think that,' I remarked, 'but we do have to rely on members of the public to help us—such as giving a description of the person they suspect.'

'I told you I didn't see him, not proper. I thought . . .'

'Well, you give all the facts to the sergeant here and we'll see what we can do.'

Alderson reached for a sheet of paper and began writing. I went out on a routine inquiry. It was nearly an hour later when I got back and the woman had gone, leaving Alderson looking a mere shadow of his former self.

'I've only just managed to get rid of her,' he said.

'What a time I've had, Bill. You'd have thought it was a bank hold-up. Not,' he added, 'but what losing four pounds ten and six isn't a serious matter to a widow woman living on a pension and a bit of cleaning. The trouble is she didn't see the fella she thinks did it, so we probably haven't a cat in hell's chance of ever putting him down.'

I said: 'Getting evidence against a dipper is about the hardest job we ever have.'

'You're right there, Bill—which reminds me that the crime sheet has too many unsolved cases of pickpocketing, a lot of 'em bigger ones than old Mrs. Hancock's purse.'

'That's a fact,' I assented. 'It is a wonder more villains don't take to dipping. Unless a man is caught in the act, which doesn't happen very often, we've precious small chance of ever putting him down.'

'Even when we *know* a fella's dipping,' added Alderson.

'True. Like Scotch Jimmy.'

'That's right. Now *there's* a case in point. He must've dipped into some of the fattest wallets in the city and we've never been able to prove a thing.'

I nodded and went into the C.I.D. room to collect some papers. On my way home I had to pass the Adelphi Hotel and remembered that a big social function was on. A car passed me, going the other way—and I caught sight of the driver. A slim, smartly dressed young fellow pushing thirty. Angus James MacCracken, art dealer and gentleman of leisure—otherwise, Scotch Jimmy.

He saw me, too, and cruised to a halt. I stopped my own car, got out and strolled across the street, which was reasonably quiet at this time. It was then that I noticed he was wearing a dinner jacket under his dark topcoat. He had wound down the window and was beaming at me. 'Why, hello, Mr. P—nice seeing you.'

'I see you're all got up like a dog's dinner,' I said genially. 'Going somewhere?'

'A night out, as you might say, Mr. P.'

I grinned at him. 'You wouldn't be going to that do at the Adelphi, by any chance?'

His smooth boyish face smiled blandly. 'As a matter of fact, no. I'm on my way to meet a very nice young lady and take her to dinner.'

'But not at the Adelphi?'

'As you say, not at the Adelphi. What made you mention that, anyway?'

'Lots of well-heeled folk will be there tonight.'

'You don't say?'

'Give over, Jimmy,' I said. 'In the last few years you've attended scores of posh do's up and down the city and even out in the country.'

'Well, tain't no sin,' he remarked cheerfully. 'Besides, I had invitations to most of them, through my art-gallery connections.'

I looked hard at him. A pleasant, smiling young fellow with one of those open countenances that inspire instant trust, though I knew he wasn't to be trusted within reaching distance of anything which looked like loot and hadn't previously been nailed down.

'You've done pretty well for yourself since you came to our town,' I mused.

'I can't complain. My little gallery attracts a lot of clients.'

'I wasn't thinking of your tin-pot gallery,' I grunted. 'What you make out of that wouldn't keep you in brass washers.'

For a few moments he didn't answer. Then he said, as if he had made his mind up about something: 'Let's go and have a drink. I've something to tell you.'

'I thought you were meeting a bird?'

He shrugged carelessly. 'Perhaps I am and perhaps I'm not. What the hell? Let's go somewhere and have that drink together.'

'All right. I'll have to park my car off this street, though. You, too.'

Five minutes later we were in a bar near Central Station. He ordered two large Scotches and said: 'I *was* going to that affair at the Adelphi, but I'll not bother now.'

'Because of seeing me, you mean?'

'Partly that, but there's something else. That's what I want to tell you about, Mr. P. I'm leaving Liverpool and going back to Scotland. My brother, who helps me with the gallery, is coming with me.'

'Well,' I said facetiously, 'that ought to be a relief to a lot of people, even if they don't realise the connection.'

'Yes.' He sipped his drink, leaned back against the padded bench seat and went on: 'You're on to me, of course. You know all about me, about how I make my money.'

'Unfortunately, I've never been able to get evidence that'd convict you, or even enable us to make a charge,' I said.

'In the end you'd have done it,' he replied soberly. 'You know something? I've been scared of you more than of any other cop in the city. Once I felt sure you'd got me in a corner, but I managed to wriggle out of it.'

'If you'd had a police record I could have held you on suspicion, loitering with intent, or something like that. Jimmy.'

'Och, that I know, so I'm not pushing my luck too far. I'm retiring.'

I chuckled. 'Retiring? That's a good word.'

'Aye, it usually means retiring after a long and honourable life and getting a gold watch handed to you with a lot of false words and happen a wee bit pension. Well, I'm retiring after a very brief and highly prosperous career and if I want a gold watch I can buy a hundred.'

'I don't doubt that.'

He looked at me coolly. 'And there's nothing you can do about it, is there?'

'Not a thing.'

'You suspected me almost from the start. You've always known I was a dipper. But it doesn't matter now. I'll never pick another pocket, so you'll not even have a chance of booking me. I'm going back home to Bonnie Scotland and ye'll no see me ever again.'

'And that's all you wanted to tell me?'

'Not all,' Scotch Jimmy said. 'Since it makes no difference now, one way or the other. I'll tell you just how I came to be a dipper, that's if you're interested.'

'I can't arrest you on the strength of a purely private conversation, which you'd naturally deny anyway, so go right ahead,' I said. 'But why tell me?'

He raised his glass like a toast. 'I've always had a sneaking affection for you, if you must know, Mr. P.'

'Thanks.'

'Och, I'm dead serious, I tell you. It just happens that I like you personally.'

'I don't actively dislike you,' I said, 'even though I know damned well that you're the biggest dipper in the city.'

'And, like I say, not a thing to be done about it,' he said merrily.

'No, I'm sorry to say. If there was I'd do it right here and now, even though you are an engaging young devil.'

He laughed, then his face became serious. 'I wasn't always a dipper,' he rejoined. 'I came to Liverpool ten years ago full of the dreams and ambitions of youth. Just a raw country lad from the Highlands with straw in my hair, like they say. Then something happened to change my entire way of life.'

'What?'

'Don't rush me, Mr. P. I'm telling you how I came to be a dipper and I'm going to tell you in my own time.'

'You have the floor, Jimmy,' I said.

'Well now, it was this way . . .' began Scotch Jimmy.

II

You may be surprised to hear it, but I'm really a stonemason (he began). I mean that's what I was trained to be up in Scotland. But jobs weren't all that easy to come by—and, anyway, I reckoned I could earn better money down here among the heathen Sassenachs.

So—picture a fine upstanding young fellow coming up to his twentieth year. That's me, Angus James MacCracken, stepping off the train and seeing the lights of Lime Street for the first time.

I'd arrived to work on the new Roman Catholic Cathedral, wearing a blue serge suit (the only one to my name) and carrying a cheap imitation-leather suitcase containing my working togs, underwear and a pair of flannel trousers. And, of course, a few toilet things. A clean, neat young chap ready to start a new life.

The first problem was to get somewhere to rest my innocent head. Well, that's not quite right—it wasn't really a problem because I'd got a couple of addresses. One was within walking distance, the other meant a tram ride. So, being a canny Scots lad, I walked. If I'd plunged threepence on car fare a lot of things would never have happened and you'd not be sat here in this pub talking to me now, Mr. P.

Well, it turned out to be a bedsitter in an old sort of

rambling house belonging to an old fella named McIverty. From Dublin he was, but he'd lived in Liverpool that long he even had the accent. He had a fine head of wavy grey hair and merry blue eyes. We got on like a house on fire, as the saying is. I've got a wee bit of a sense of humour, as I dare say you've noticed, and this old fella was fair bubbling with it.

After a while it got like he was a father to me. He started taking me on trips with him—New Brighton, Rhyl Colwyn Bay, Llandudno, up to Blackpool in the season. He explained that his work took him there and when we arrived he'd disappear for a few hours. Then we'd meet for a high tea in one of the best cafés in the place before catching the train home.

I began to wonder just what kind of work old Mack, as I called him, actually did. You see, he'd never so much as given me a hint of what it was. So one night when we were having a drink in a boozer near Central Station up in Blackpool, I asked him point-blank.

For a moment Mack's merry face went serious. But he never could stay like that for long. The twinkle came back in his eyes and he said after taking a very careful look round: 'Well now, I s'pose I'll have to tell you . . . I'm a dipper.'

'A *what*?'

He looked at his handsome gold watch. 'The train leaves in ten minutes—I'll tell you on the way to the station.'

In fact, he kept up a running fire of humorous comments until we'd taken our seats in a compartment and he'd made sure nobody else was getting in. Then, as the train pulled out, he looked keenly across at me and said: 'A dipper or dip is slang for a pickpocket. I'm one.'

I gaped at him. 'You're telling me you *rob* people?'

'Ah, 'tis a hard way of putting it,' quoth he. 'I prefer

to say that I relieve the well-to-do of a little spare cash.'

'But . . . but that's dishonest,' I said. It seemed a stupid thing to say.

The twinkle in his eyes was replaced by a worried look—the first time I'd ever seen one on his genial face. 'I hope this isn't going to change our friendly relationship, Jimmy,' he said.

To tell you the truth, I was fair shocked. But I was also excited—and curious. I'd heard about pickpockets and had read notices in public places warning you to watch out for them, but I'd never met one or ever thought I would. And all the time I'd been living in a house belonging to one.

'I couldn't get vexed with you, Mack,' I said. 'But I must say it's a surprise.' A thought struck me and I went on: 'It must take a hell of a lot of nerve.'

He chuckled. 'Ah, you get used to it,' he said.

'I'm blessed if I know how you get away with it,' I reflected.

'You have to learn the craft, like any other.'

Another thought sprang up in my head and without stopping even to ponder it I said: 'Show me!'

'Well,' he answered soberly. 'I don't know about that. You've got a respectable job and I wouldn't want to set your feet on the downward path, like.'

'Hell, Mack, I wasn't thinking of joining you—I'd just like to see how it's done.'

He hesitated, but not for long. One of the facts of life is that all experts are eager to demonstrate their knowledge and skills, and old Mack was no exception. In the course of the next few weeks he taught me all he knew about the dubious art of picking pockets, and what he knew was plenty. I think he simply wanted to show me how clever he was. In the event, he taught me the game.

But I still had not even the smallest intention of putting

this knowledge to practical purpose. So far as I was concerned, it was some sort of amusing game.

That is, until I set off for Scotland for a holiday with my parents and younger brother. I hadn't been home for nearly a year and I was really looking forward to it. I had quite a bit of money on me—thirty-seven quid, to be exact.

Well, I had to change trains at Carlisle. I had more than a full hour to wait and decided to take a stroll round the town. My railway ticket was in my wallet and when I got back to the station with five minutes to spare I put my hand in my pocket for it.

The wallet had gone. . .

So there I was stranded in Carlisle without a penny. I remembered that I'd been in a pub for a pint and that some fella had brushed against me. I didn't even see him properly before, with a hasty apology, he disappeared.

It was only too painfully clear what had happened. I'd been dipped. I stood on the wrong side of the station barrier and watched the night express come in and go out. I was desperate. I turned away and glanced at my wristwatch. It was twenty-five minutes to ten. The pubs were still open. I drew one long, deep breath and set off for them.

It was the hard, inescapable fact that I'd been robbed of all my humble savings that gave me the will and the courage to put into actual use all the cunning techniques Mack had painstakingly taught me. It was a craft I had never for one moment expected to use. But circumstances alter cases, don't they?

I worked fast, moving from bar to bar. Not to beat about the bush, I finished up with seventy-nine pounds, seven ten shilling notes and a postal order made out to a football pools firm. I went back to the railway station, got my suitcase out of the left luggage office and checked in at the best hotel in the place as cool as dammit. I thought to myself: 'I'm made for life!'

The next morning I bought a first- class ticket to Glasgow and hired a car to get to the village where my folks lived. Nothing but the best now! I had a grand holiday—even the sun shone brilliantly all the time. Then I returned to Liverpool, and handed in my notice. The work on the new Cathedral would have to get along without Angus James MacCracken. I was a dip.

On those trips we made (when he had so conveniently vanished for a few hours) Mack had used the services of a confederate. This fella is known as a passer—as you well know, Mr. P. The dipper picks a pocket and immediately hands the wallet or purse to the passer, who instantly beats it. So if, by some sad mischance, the dipper is accused by the victim—why, he has nothing incriminating on him. Not a sausage!

At first, I worked with Mack—and also alone. Finally, I sent for my brother Donald . . . and to cut a long story short we teamed up. Yes, I know what you're thinking, Mr. P. That we've become the finest team of dippers in the city. Well, it's not for me to boast, so all I'll say is that we've done a lot more than well out of it.

Old Mack—he's gone now, God rest him—taught us even more tricks of the trade. I tell you he was that pleased with our progress you'd have thought he'd come into a fortune or something. Mind you, he didn't have any cause for complaint, especially when he got older, because we looked after him all right.

We set up my nice little art gallery just to have a legitimate business front, and also because it helped give us contacts. Believe me, we've had a right run for our money—or rather other fellas' money! Holidays in Italy and on the Costa del Sol, a new car every twelve months, money in the bank and investments.

Where did we dip? Ah, you know well enough. Hotels, social functions, the poshest bars, big stores, markets, fairs—and, to be sure, all those nice cosy jaunts to the popular seaside resorts when the money-loaded crowds are there.

Mind you, we sometimes had our little problems. Like the time we went to a big country market. By noon the main pub was crowded with farmers knocking back their pints and their shorts. Farmers always crack on about the bad harvest or something, but I never saw one without the price of a round of drinks and a car to drive off home in.

But I was telling you of this particular case. We had our eye on one farmer in particular. He had a wallet thick enough to choke a horse, but he kept it in his trousers pocket with his left hand in it all the time, except when he was paying for a round. It seemed hopeless—not even an expert dipper can hope to nick a wallet if the fella keeps his hand on it.

Then I got an idea. It was simple really, and I don't know why I didn't think of it right away. Still, better late than never, as they say. You see, there was a group of us drinking at the bar. All farmers except me and Donald, but we'd sort of joined them and everybody was in a mellow mood—most of them were half-cut, in fact.

So while Donald engaged this particular farmer in conversation—telling him an off-colour joke, actually—I lit a cigarette and accidentally-on-purpose burned the farmer's left ear. Up came his left hand out of his pocket and in went mine. It was done in a flash—his wallet out and another (stuffed with worthless paper) in its place. Then, in the general rumpus of talk and leg-pulling, we quietly sidled out. A few minutes later we were on separate buses leaving town. You never make the mistake of using your own car—some fella might remember the number. Also—always split up, it makes for much greater safety.

The only time we ever ran into a spot of bother was during Scotch Week in the Isle of Man when we got mixed up in a shindy with the Glasgow mob and were slung into the local cells. Then we found we'd run out of cigarettes. Twenty minutes later we had a new packet of twenty ... we dipped the warder! I've always thought of that little incident as a highlight of my career.

Well, it all began with old Mack, but I don't suppose for a moment I'd ever have turned dip except for having my own pocket picked all those years ago on Carlisle station. Ten years ago, in fact. I never worked again. We've lived well and at this very minute I calculate we're worth quite a few quid—between us I mean.

And now it's all over and finished. You'll not have any more trouble from us, Mr. P. I just thought you'd like to know ...

III

I looked at Scotch Jimmy for what was indeed to be the last time. An engaging young scoundrel, but still a scoundrel. I thought of all that he and his brother had done ... of the countless wallets and purses illegally transferred to their possession.

It was difficult to dislike Scotch Jimmy. He was the big dipper and richly deserved retribution—the retribution I was unable to arrange simply because I hadn't so much as a tithe of admissible evidence—but he was not vicious. No person had ever suffered violence at his hands and his nature was as warm and friendly as the most fastidious could wish.

I prefer my true-life stories to have a good moral ending—in the apprehension and just punishment of the miscreants involved in it, no matter how engaging they may be. At the same time, I like to think that at least some of the knaves will reform.

And Scotch Jimmy did. Well, of course, you may say he could afford to, and this I cannot deny.

I asked him what his plans were when he and his brother returned to the mountainous and majestic land of their birth.

'We've bought a grand farm and we aim to settle down as the genial squires of the village, Mr. P,' he said buoyantly.

That was nineteen years ago. Last summer I was motoring in Scotland and stopped for lunch in a certain village. In the cocktail lounge I could not avoid overhearing several cordial references to the most prosperous farming brothers in the neighbourhood.

I ventured a few inquiries and learned the names of the two squires who were so much revered by one and all. Little did the good folk up there know—and it was no business of mine to enlighten them.

They wouldn't have believed me, anyway . . .

7

A Day by the Sea

Kitty McBride was sitting by the hearth in her little home. It was high summer, so there was no fire. Not that Kitty would have found it easy to light one anyway, because she was skint.

And to make matters worse, the annual Lodge Picnic to Blackpool was to take place in a couple of days' time. The cost of a return ticket on the coach, plus coffee on the way up and a figure-filling high tea beside the seaside, was thirty bob . . . but it might as well have been thirty quid, for all the chance Kitty could see of laying her hands on it.

A fine buxom woman was Kitty McBride with a broad smiling face and a ready laugh which, in moments of alcoholic exuberance, sounded not unlike the Scotch express going through a tunnel. Not that Kitty was an alcoholic; she was just a big strong woman who liked bottles of stout and congenial company.

All her mates were going on the trip and if she failed to turn up an inevitable loss of face must ensue. A minor matter? To you and me perhaps it would be; but in the circles in which Kitty moved it was neither more nor less than a humiliation too great to be borne. Tongues would wag, remarks would be made behind her back—or, worse, even in her presence. To put the matter simply, absence from the annual outing would lower her prestige for at least a year and thus was something not to be borne by a proud spirit.

But how to raise the price? It was a problem which pressed grievously upon her. She could, of course, pay a visit to Jenny Brocklehurst, the back-street moneylender who organised the trip. After all, Kitty had been there often enough in the recent past, borrowing £2 on Monday and paying it back out of the Public Assistance money on the Friday, plus 4s. interest. But relations between Kitty and Mrs. Brocklehurst had lately been somewhat less than cordial and Kitty was in no mood to play the supplicant, especially at those rates of interest.

True, she had a husband. But it was no good asking Jim since he hadn't worked for years. 'It's me chest, you see, luv,' wheezed Jim over the fag-end which was invariably glued to his mouth. 'It's me poor ould chest, loike, that's stopping a hard-working fella from doin' anything.'

Notwithstanding his enfeebled condition, the instant Jim laid hands on his dole money he was in the boozers like a sparrow on the nest. In fact, the only way Kitty could get a share for the housekeeping was by waylaying him as he stepped jauntily out of the Labour Exchange.

Well, the more she brooded over the situation the more hopeless it seemed. In fact, Kitty was getting to the point at which she would be forced, in sheer desperation, to visit Jenny Brocklehurst—thus getting further in her toils.

Then, suddenly from out of nowhere, an idea emerged, blooming like an expanding rose under warm sun. The more Kitty McBride looked at it, the more masterly it appeared. It involved a series of deals beside which the puny operations of vast cartels and take-over bids looked like small fry; but, in the basic essence, it was simplicity itself.

Kitty wasted no time. She grabbed her hat and coat and made a bee-line for the well-known pawnbroking establishment of one Billy Gratton. She let herself in through the back entrance, an unobtrusive move entirely seemly to one who had been a customer for years. In fact, she was even better known at Billy Gratton's than in the saloon bars she frequented, which is saying a very great deal.

'Hi, Kitty,' intoned Billy. 'And what can I be doing for you?'

Kitty leaned her splendid figure against the pitted counter. 'You can do me a real favour, Billy boy,' she said.

Billy Gratton's eyes, though continuing to twinkle, now had a wary look as well. 'Well . . . er . . .' he began carefully.

'It's just to help my old man,' went on Kitty. 'He's got a job.'

Billy Gratton clutched at the counter for support. The statement seemed to be more than his frail strength could bear. 'He's *what*?' croaked Billy feebly.

'Ah, 'tis right enough,' cried Kitty. 'A light job, mind you, on account of all the trouble he has with his chest.'

'Well, I'm glad to know Jim's going to work for you at last,' said Billy, 'but what d'you expect me to do?'

' 'Tis a pair of trousers he needs,' answered Kitty. 'Not a decent pair to his name. He can't start a new job with his shirt hanging out now, can he?'

'H'm,' said Billy Gratton.

'Two pairs on appro and I'll pay when I come back with the pair he doesn't suit, how about that?'

'I'm none so sure . . .'

'Ah, come on now. You'll not want to stop my Jim starting work at long last.'

'Why don't he come hisself then?' demanded Billy.

Kitty was ready for that, or anything else. 'He's in bed, it's that chest of his, like I said.'

Billy Gratton pondered for a moment, then made the great decision. After all, Kitty was a regular and so deserving of consideration, especially in the unique circumstances. He got down a couple of pairs of trousers, twenty-nine inch inside leg measurement, thirty-four inch round the middle, and silently handed them over.

'And mind you're back in quick-sticks, Kitty,' he admonished.

'I'll be back so fast you'll hardly know I've been gone,' called Kitty. There was a pleased smile on her good-looking face as she stepped out on to the pavement. She was already more than half-way to the price, but there were a few more cards that must be played if all was to go according to plan.

She walked swiftly up the street to the main road and dived into another pawnshop. Three minutes later she had pawned one pair of pants for 10s. Now she nipped on to a bus. A ride of only a couple of stages brought her to her next stopping-point, a third pawnbroker's establishment. The second pair of pants went up the proverbial spout.

With one lovely quid in her purse Kitty hopped on another bus. She could have executed her master strategy on foot, but time was important. Her destination was a credit drapery, a new store in the locality. The way this type of business works is that you are issued with a check entitling you to buy goods up to the value of £5 in any local drapery emporium. You pay this off at the rate of 5s. weekly, with a 10 per cent poundage for the facility.

With a fine flourish Kitty signed the required form and the bottom half—representing the entitlement to purchase—was handed to her. Ten minutes later she was in a shop buying two wool blankets, two sheets and a brace of pillow-cases. Bang went the £5 voucher.

Armed with these possessions, Kitty took a bus to a better part of the city and pawned the lot for £4 at a higher-class establishment. Then—back to the two pawnbrokers where she had pledged the two pairs of trousers. These she immediately redeemed, explaining—which was only too true—that she had unexpectedly found she didn't need the money.

Finally, she fetched up again at Billy Gratton's.

'You've not been long, luv,' said he. Then his eyes popped as Kitty laid not one but both pairs of trousers on the counter. 'What's to do?' he asked.

'My old fella's changed his mind, he reckons he ain't fit to take the job after all. . . .'

Billy chuckled. 'I thought it was too good to be true, Jim McBride actually going to *work*,' he said. As a matter of fact, Billy was more than a bit relieved to see her. He had already begun to harbour doubts about his wisdom in allowing Kitty to take anything out of his shop without first parting with money. And that tale she had told about her old fella going to work. He wondered how he had ever believed it. To the best of his knowledge and belief, Jim McBride would want a job carrying swansdown before he consented to go to work.

'Aye, he's got a lazy bone in his back, never mind the trouble he says he has with his chest,' joked Kitty. 'And me having to go out cleaning to keep the roof over our poor heads.'

Billy Gratton eyed her for a moment, then said: ' 'Tis powerful hard on a woman being saddled with a fella like Jim, but you cert'nly don't look starved.'

'I do me best, Billy Gratton,' said Kitty. 'And don't you go making low sneaky remarks about my Jim.'

'I only thought he was a work-shy . . .'

'Happen he is, but I'm not thanking *you* to say it,'

retorted Kitty, and left with a fine swish of skirts.

Now came the crowning moment. The moment of confrontation. She could hardly wait to slip it across Jenny Brocklehurst. But there was no smirking triumph on Kitty's face as she swept into the moneylender's parlour. Just a gracious air, such as might be made by a grand dame of the old school about to condescend towards one of plebeian origin.

But Mrs. Brocklehurst knew nothing of this and was too wrapped up in private gloating to sense the subtle change in her erstwhile client's demeanour. 'She's come to barrow the price of the trip,' was what Jenny told herself. 'Ah, well, th' interest'll be higher for keeping me waiting!'

She fiddled with the ornate cameo brooch on her ample bosom and said carelessly: 'Come to borrow a wee bit money for t'trip, have you, Kitty me darling?'

Kitty smiled her most winning smile. 'That I have not,' she said even more carelessly. 'I've merely come to buy a ticket and I wouldn't buy it here if there was any other way!'

As she spoke she spread a £1 note and a 10s note on the table. Jenny Brocklehurst's eyes bulged like twin golf balls and her jaw sagged about three inches off the parent hinges. Her mouth moved but no words came. The spectacle of Kitty McBride paying in advance for anything appeared to have temporarily robbed her of the power of speech.

When she recovered it she croaked: 'Have you enough for ale, Kitty? I could let you have a wee bit . . .'

'Keep it, you old baggage,' said Kitty loftily. 'I've drawn from me savings what I have in t'Post Office and swore never to touch. But I wasn't going to borrow, least of all off you, Jenny Brocklehurst. So I'll just trouble you to hand over that ticket . . .'

Jenny marked her down on the list, handed the ticket over and made one last gallant stand. 'Ye'll need a wee bit for new clothes, won't you?' she said.

'I'm quite well fixed, thank you,' said Kitty. And indeed she was, though it would scarcely have been politic to explain how this agreeable state of affairs came about. In fact, the house where she went cleaning three days a week belonged to a comfortably-off young couple who chanced to be holidaying over in Killarney. They had left the key with Kitty, so what more natural than to try the young wife's spare clothes on in front of the wardrobe mirror and select something appropriate for the great occasion? In passing, I should tell you that Kitty was having all the luck because the young wife was a fine buxom lass, too.

In the event, Kitty selected the most vivid costume available, for it was her intention not merely to cut a bit of a dash in a general way but to strike Jenny Brocklehurst literally green with envy and suppressed rage. Many were the insinuations Kitty had had to endure from the grasping old moneylender, and it seemed to her that this was the time to settle a few scores.

The coach left at 8.30 next morning and Mrs. Brocklehurst rolled up in all her flamboyant finery, looking like Mulligan's goose. But when she cast eyes on Kitty she nearly had a relapse. For here was expensive elegance which Jenny Brocklehurst simply couldn't match or account for. And the admiring tributes of Kitty's mates was like salt in an open wound. It pretty well ruined Mrs. Brocklehurst's journey to the celebrated resort. However, on the return journey, mellowed by fattening food and almost soluble with ale, Jenny was in a better mood. As for Kitty, her face was split in two by a smile which looked half a mile wide.

And this wasn't entirely because she had had the best

day out within living memory. There was another little matter which she was prudently keeping to herself.

'When the credit drapery collector calls on Jenny Brocklehurst for the first weekly five bob payment oh, what a to-do there's going to be,' thought Kitty.

For she had signed Jenny Brocklehurst's name and address to the £5 clothing check . . .

II

A quiet peaceful morning in City Police Headquarters. No desk telephones ringing, no urgent calls from the patrolling Z-cars, no testy complaints from oppressed members of the public. I lit a cigarette and ordered tea from the canteen. By the time I was able to drink it the stuff had gone cold.

Mrs. Jenny Brocklehurst was in our midst. You could pretty well say she erupted in our midst. So great was her emotion that she appeared to be in imminent danger of blowing up.

'It's a disgrace, that's what it is!' she shrieked. 'What are t'police for, any road?'

'Well,' I said soberly, 'you ought to know the answer to that.'

She was swelling visibly, like a captive balloon, when I started speaking. But my words deflated her. 'What's that supposed to mean?' she said uncertainly.

I could have told her, but the fact was we had no proof of what we suspected: i.e. that in addition to lending money at fancy rates of interest, she was doing a small but not unrewarding business on the side as a fence.

'Nothing, Mrs. Brocklehurst,' I said. 'Kindly state the nature of your complaint, if you have one.'

Finally, we got out of her the fact that her name had

been signed to a £5 drapery check and that she suspected the hand of Kitty McBride.

'Proof,' I said patiently, 'how about proof?'

'Well, the collector's never laid eyes on the brazen baggage, but she went to the shop in person.'

'You mean the fella who made out the check can identify her?'

Another look came on her cunning face. 'Well, I'm none so sure,' she admitted vexedly. 'The fella there is a wee bit short-sighted and might not have got a proper look at her. On t'other hand, he'd know her voice, I dare say?'

'It doesn't sound much to go on, Mrs. Brocklehurst. Are you making a charge against Kitty McBride?'

Her eyes became even more cunning. 'That's for you lot, int it?' she demanded. 'T'police can make charges once they get some evvydence, can't they?'

'It's been known,' I agreed.

I had small trouble finding Kitty McBride. She had moved to a new housing estate, doing what is known as a moonlight in the process. This is a way of saying that a person moves his or her furniture and belongings at dead of night, leaving no forwarding address, thus causing alarm and despondency in the breasts of all creditors.

When I tracked her down after several days of asking round, she was delighted to see me.

'I hear you've been a bad girl, Kitty,' I admonished.

She widened her merry blue eyes. 'Who, me? Why I never heard of such a thing.'

'Mrs. Brocklehurst the well-known neighbourhood money-lender, thinks you put her name to a five-pound drapery check and is screaming the place down,' I went on. 'You can hear her from Fairfield to the East Lancs Road and back.'

Kitty was standing with her hands splayed on her

ample hips. Now she fairly shook with laughter.

I stared out of the window at the rows of small new houses. There were acres of roads like this one, and they were likely to present more than a little trouble to the C.I.D. I knew that dotted about here and there would be a few, or even more than a few, tearaways, looking for easy pickings when householders were down at the local or out in their cars bought on the never-never. And what Kitty McBride didn't already know or could find out about everyone in the district was liable to be nobody's business. She had tipped me off in the past.

Besides, I couldn't see much hope of getting a conviction over that £5 check signature. On the other hand, it wasn't for me to tell Kitty that, much as I liked her.

'Instead,' I said gravely: 'Suppose I do a little deal with you? You keep me informed about all suspicious comings and goings in the neighbourhood and I'll close the book on this bit of a moan Jenny Brocklehurst is making.'

'Done!' cried Kitty jubilantly.

'There's one other thing, though,' I said.

'Ah now, what's that then?'

'Tell me just what really happened about that day at the seaside you had and how you managed to pay for it . . . I like a good laugh as well as the next man.'

I got it.

8

A Smile for the Angry Cat

It was periodically necessary for some members of the C.I.D. to bring Teddy Low along for interviewing. This was partly because Teddy was well known as a professional thief and also because he invariably betrayed his handiwork.

Of course, all *modus operandi* men tend to put their trade mark on their work, but Teddy stood out like a sore thumb owing to his ingrained addiction to stealing overcoats.

Now you may well think that lifting other people's topcoats when their backs are turned is an unrewarding occupation, but Teddy make quite a thing out of it. To start with, it was his resolute custom to pinch only the very best overcoats—and, secondly, it is surprising but true that more than a few people leave money in overcoat pockets. Teddy frequently found £1 and £5 notes, sometimes even wallets.

But finding money in the coats was a sort of bonus; he made his living selling the coats off all round the city and its suburbs. If you are enterprising enough you can knock off anything up to a dozen or so coats in a day, netting anything from two to five or six quid a time. Over a week this adds up and it's tax free.

Teddy operated in all the best places, specially favouring the men's rooms in the best hotels and restaurants—

though, mind you, he had even been known to lift these garments out of office blocks. Of course, in the summer business was non-existent and he had to try something else—but at the time this story opened winter was upon us.

There was one other peculiarity about Teddy Low. I well remember a young detective constable questioning him for the first time and being fascinated by what happened. You will have observed a cat crouching on its hind legs and spitting? Well, that's exactly what Teddy Low did when you asked him to explain something. Then he invariably demanded: 'Who wants to know?' This strange habit, which he never lost, got him the nickname of the Angry Cat—except among those Jacks who, struck by his pale and skinny appearance, dubbed him the Ghost.

But to most of us Teddy Low was always the Angry Cat. Even when not being pulled in for questioning about this or that suspected misdemeanour, he was seldom to be seen wearing a smile.

But I was going to tell you a story about Teddy. For a couple of weeks we had been receiving complaints about overcoats vanishing and, not unnaturally, suspicion fell on him. But he had changed his last known address, and though Z-cars and ordinary foot-slogging coppers had been told to keep their eyes wide open, none had so far caught even a fleeting glimpse of him.

Then, early on a chill November evening, the telephone rang. Sam Goodyard picked up the instrument with no premonition of the sensational news he was about to hear.

'Goodyard speaking ...' He paused and a stricken look came on his finely chiselled features. 'You ... you mean ... incredible . . . I beg your pardon, sir, of course

I don't doubt it . . . very good, sir . . . I'll put our best men on to it . . . yes, sir . . .'

He put the receiver back on its rest with a palsied hand and turned towards me.

'Has the Lord Mayor been foully done to death?' I inquired facetiously.

'You're almost right, Bill, but not quite,' the D.I. replied. 'His overcoat has been nicked.'

'You don't say.'

'And it's no laughing matter, I can tell you,' said Sam. 'The Lord Mayor's best Sunday-go-to-meeting overcoat it is. He's been on to the Chief Con and the Chief Con has just been on to me. Demanding instant action by all men on the strength and swift retribution to the malefactor.'

'The Angry Cat again,' I said. 'Only Teddy would think of strolling into a civic event and calmly walking off with the Lord Mayor's topcoat.'

'Get him!' rapped the D.I. 'Grab him or we'll be in dead lumber—worse than with a murder case.'

I sighed. 'We'd have booked the Cat days ago but for the fact that we seem totally unable to find him.'

Goodyard grunted. 'Look, he must be somewhere in the city. Try again, it doesn't matter if it takes all night.'

'Doesn't matter to whom?' I said. 'I'm just going off duty.'

'You're joking, of course,' grinned Sam. 'You're back on duty without even having been off. Get moving, Bill, and let's have the Cat behind bars by morning, eh?'

'I wouldn't care to bet on it,' I said gloomily. 'When it comes to dodging capture, the Cat has been more than well named.'

I went out with Z Victor Two. We tried all the lodging houses again. We thought of all the low dives Teddy Low could possibly be in. We even hunted up known friends and his few relatives. He was nowhere to be seen, and nobody knew where he was . . . or, if they did know, they weren't letting on.

Other officers had checked every second-hand dealer in the city. They returned with an impressive collection of stolen topcoats, but the Lord Mayor's wasn't one of them. So far as we could make out, the Angry Cat hadn't even tried to flog it.

For the next few days the Chief Constable was frequently on the phone, prompted by the Lord Mayor, but we had nothing which even looked like progress to report.

'We're one of the great police forces in the country and we can't recover the Lord Mayor's overcoat,' said the Chief sourly. 'It's fortunate we're not being called upon just now to arrest a bank robber.'

Now this was an odd remark because less than a week later we were being required to do exactly that. A message came through that a man had held up a bank near Bold Street and got away with £2,700. We were given a description of the man, but it didn't seem to fit anyone on the police file.

Then another message arrived . . . suspect believed travelling on night boat to Isle of Man. I went down to the Pierhead with Detective Constable Blake. By the time the boat was due to sail for Douglas we hadn't seen anyone answering to the description. So we sailed, too.

Bright and early next morning I was sauntering on the main deck when I spotted in the distance a figure which was at once familiar yet strikingly different. I quickened my stride, caught up with him and said: 'Good morning to you!'

The figure turned. It was none other than the Angry Cat. He went into his back-on-the-hind-legs routine and a spitting sound came from him.

'What d'yer want, then?' he asked when he had recovered.

I looked him over from stem to stern. Never had the Cat presented so flawless an appearance. From his polished black Oxfords to his well-cut blue suit, crisp white shirt, solid blue tie and curly-brimmed felt hat he was like a male model. But the *coup de grâce* was given by the magnificent forty-guinea overcoat, lately the property of the Lord Mayor of Liverpool.

'What I want is two things—you and the stolen coat you're wearing,' I said sternly.

For an instant I got the idea that he was going to run for it. I chuckled and said: 'No use dashing off, Cat. You're on board ship and there's nowhere to go, unless you fancy a dip in the Irish Sea.'

He shivered as if he could feel the cold embrace of those tossing grey waters. Then he sighed and said: 'It's a fair cop. I shouldn't have kept that coat—but, to tell you the truth, I took a right fancy to it.'

'The Lord Mayor fancies it even more,' I said, 'though whether he'll still fancy it when he discovers whose back it's been on is another thing.'

The Cat drew himself up haughtily. 'I'm clean, Mr. P,' he protested. 'I had a bath in Chester last night and another one when I got up this morning.'

I eyed him curiously. 'Chester,' I mused. 'Is that where you've been these last few days?'

'There and Colwyn Bay, Mr. P. Sort of keeping out of harm's way.'

'So that's why we couldn't find you. We should have alerted all police forces, but we were sure you were still in Liverpool. Still, Nemesis has finally caught up with you.'

'Who?'

'Never mind,' I said. 'The point is that you're under arrest.'

The jaunty look faded from him.

'You don't mean I'll not be allowed to land at Douglas!' he moaned.

'You'll be able to land all right, but only to be lodged in the local cells until we're ready to return, I'm afraid.'

'And me just going after a job in the island . . .'

'What job?'

'I've got an interview with a fella who's in Douglas with the idea of opening a funfair next season, sideshow stalls, you know the kind of thing, Mr. P. He arranged for me to see him on the mainland, but I thought a trip on the ocean wave would do me good . . .'

'And the island is a long way from Liverpool, eh?'

'Well, that, too. But look . . . have a heart and let me keep this appointment. Then you can take me back.'

'H'm,' I said, 'you might well be in Walton when the next summer season opens. Let's see, it's November now. You might get twelve months, less a bit of remission for good conduct. Even so, you might not be out in time to take that job.'

'I'd like to keep faith with this fella just the same,' argued Teddy.

'All right, then.'

The Cat shook my hand. 'You're a real nice Jack, Mr. P. Besides, it'd be a shame not to keep the appointment after I've got meself all dressed up for it.'

'There is that,' I admitted. 'I see you're wearing some very smart clothes apart from the Lord Mayor's overcoat. Where'd you get them?'

He grinned. 'Well, I don't mind telling you,' he offered. 'I nip into a tailoring shop at lunchtime when there's only one fella on duty and him a beginner. I tell him I'll try a suit on, which I do. Then I put my old mack on over it and walk out saying the suit wasn't just what I wanted. After I've scarpered he finds me ould shabby ruin of a suit hanging up among the new ones. Easy, eh?'

'That ought to add a couple of months to your sentence,' I growled.

'Heck, I'm sorry I told you,' he lamented.

I let the cat keep his appointment while I waited outside. He didn't try to sneak out the back way. After about twenty minutes he came out and reported that he had landed the job. 'Even if the beaks prevent me taking it when the season opens, I've kept faith with this fella and can have the job in the following summer,' he reported. 'I made quite an impression on him.'

'I'll bet you did,' I said drily.

Meanwhile, it had occurred to me that that description we had been given of the bank raider must have been a faulty one. This did not greatly surprise me; eyewitnesses are not always reliable in describing what they have seen with their own eyes—which explains why three different citizens reporting an accident will often give as many distinct versions. We did not even know for certain if the raider had come over on the boat—though that bit of news had come to us through an informer.

I had a conference with the island police chiefs and a systematic check on all hotels and boarding-houses was arranged. Anyone who had arrived on that particular boat would be questioned. I wasn't too hopeful, though —because if the description was at fault we simply had no way of knowing whether any man we interviewed was the right man.

Detective Constable Blake was in charge of Teddy Low and shortly before tea-time I joined them in a stroll along the promenade. We were walking towards the quay just beyond Victoria Street when Teddy suddenly grabbed my arm and said: 'That fella in front . . . I know him . . .'

I glanced ahead. A heavily built man wearing a checked topcoat and carrying a small case was walking quickly towards the quay. The boat we had come on was due to put to sea in less than half an hour.

'A friend of yours?' I asked.

The Cat nodded eagerly. 'Sure, I can recognise him even from t'back. I'd just like to swap a few words. We was in stir together, he comes from Manchester and . . .'

'What was he inside for?' I said. A powerful suspicion had suddenly gripped me.

'Oh, he stuck up some bank,' replied Teddy.

'He did, eh? Well, you go right up to him, then.'

'Thanks, Mr. P.' Teddy Low trotted ahead, touched the man's arm. The fellow almost jumped clear of the ground.

'Hello, Curly . . .' But Teddy got no further. The man wheeled and started running. Either he had guessed we were detectives or, more likely, he had heard about the island police making inquiries—and was anxious to get safely on that Liverpool-bound boat.

Blake and I raced after him. The small case he was carrying was stuffed with loot. When we had him in custody I reflected that neither in physical looks nor attire did he resemble the description we had been provided with.

We were all putting out to sea when I said to Teddy Low: 'But for you we'd never have known this fellow was a hook. You've done us a service and we'll not forget it.'

The Angry Cat sighed. 'That'll be a lot of consolation when I'm doing me bit of time in Walton,' he replied lugubriously.

He came up before the court in due course, pleading

guilty to feloniously stealing one overcoat, property of the Lord Mayor. We could have made a stack of other overcoat charges. We could have read out all his previous convictions.

But we didn't and he got off with six months in the second division. Before they took him away in the plain black van I had a few words with him. 'You'll be out in good time to take that job in the island,' I said.

This time he shook both my hands. 'You've been real good to me, Mr. P,' he exclaimed. 'I'll not forget it.'

A vast smile lit up his pale features. It was the first time I had ever seen a smile on the glum face of the Angry Cat.

'What a time I'll have over in Douglas next summer,' he cried joyously.

I could readily imagine it. There would be ample opportunities for nicking the belongings of the innocent holidaymakers.

'I'll do you another good turn,' I said. 'I'll make sure you stay on the straight and narrow all next summer by having the local Jacks keep a friendly eye on you.'

The smile vanished from his face as if I had wiped it off.

'Heck!' he groaned.

I dropped a kindly hand on his shoulder. 'That's right,' I said. 'You may not think it, but your best friends are the coppers. . . .'

9

Seeing the Light

At the time of which I am writing there was no more zealous traffic cop in the city than Constable Joe Standy. He was six feet four inches tall and looked as if he had been hewn from some durable substance such as granite, which made Big Joe a commanding figure when on duty at traffic control points. But he had more than physique. Big Joe was the owner of an alert and enterprising eye for the vagaries of motorists. Nothing escaped him.

On a dark, wet night on The Drive—the big dual carriageway which sweeps across the outskirts of the city from one end to the other—the cars were streaking in an endless procession *en route* for the big Liverpool soccer match.

Big Joe was on duty at one of the intersections, expertly sifting the traffic flow, when a powerful car suddenly loomed up without lights. Up went Big Joe's hamlike hand under the centre spotlight at the teeming junction.

But even as he made the gesture it seemed to him that the driver wasn't going to stop. In the general way of things, Joe's face, though resembling a rockbound coast, is amiable . . . but now it took on a scowling grimness.

At the same time he stepped forward and planted himself solidly in the path of the oncoming offender. There was a tumultuous squeal of brakes as the motorist ground to a halt.

Joe nipped round to the offside. The window was wound down, but the driver had his face half-turned away.

As was his custom with all motorists who got out of line, Big Joe spoke as follows: 'Didn't ya see me, mister?'

Now this opening gambit invariably brought the mumbled reply: 'Well, er, no, officer . . . not at first, like.'

But on this occasion it immediately became clear that there was to be a major break with honoured tradition. For the only answer Big Joe got was a big, hard fist coming through the window like a ramrod—straight in his left eye.

The gallant officer reeled back, and before he could recover his self-possession the erring driver was going through his gears as if he were on a racing circuit, weaving in and out of the stalled traffic and then shooting down a side road.

By the time Big Joe had blown his whistle the car had vanished. It was a dilemma for Constable Joseph Henry Standy. If he took time out to operate his radio handset the traffic tangle would get into a hopeless mess; if he didn't the car would get clean away.

Then his eyes lit up—or, rather, one of them did. The other was already taking on the aspect of deep purple. A Z-car had nosed up to the front in the opposite junction and Bert Rawlings was hurrying across to find out what was happening. Big Joe explained in a few crisp sentences enlivened with telling expletives and Bert went back to the Z-car and got through to Information at Police Headquarters.

The chase was on . . . and it was to be a lot more dramatic than Big Joe Standy imagined.

II

I was in the C.I.D. room deep in conversation with Detective Inspector Sam Goodyard.

'There's a new villain at large in the manor, Bill,' the D.I. declared. 'Either a villain who's moved in here from some other part of the country, or a fella without any previous record, quite unknown to the law.'

'It looks like that,' I agreed. 'But I'm wondering about something else.'

'Oh? Such as what?'

I tapped a forefinger on the file which lay on the desk. 'Seven break-ins in a period of just over a fortnight and all in the same area—the select residential zone adjoining The Drive.'

'Well, it's a good district for a fella engaged on the old housebreaking lark. Plenty of valuables, and even plenty of money left lying about. The file indicates a total haul running out at more than four and a half thousand pounds.'

I lit a cigarette and said slowly: 'I'm wondering whether what we're up against is a gifted amateur *who actually lives in the area himself*.'

'It's a possibility, Bill . . . it would explain a number of things, not least the fact that none of the known villains seem to be implicated. And there's another factor. All these raids have the look of being done by a man of keen intelligence and observation.'

I nodded. 'I think I'll start some discreet inquiries going, specifically about anyone spending money rather too freely.'

'Yes, that might do for a beginning,' Sam Goodyard said.

I went through into the main office. Alderson, the desk

sergeant, called out: 'Bill—what do you think? Some motorist has slugged Big Joe Standy.'

'Well, well!'

'Aye, bang in the eye when Big Joe tried to question him for looking as if he was going to ignore his signal . . . and driving a car with no lights at that.'

Though sorry for Big Joe, I could not repress a smile. 'Well, it'll certainly be a new experience for Joe, a fella giving him a black eye in full view of the populace . . .' I paused. A sudden thought had struck me. 'Wait a minute —isn't Big Joe on traffic control somewhere on The Drive?'

'Yeh, that's right, near the . . .' Alderson broke off. A uniformed constable had entered with a slip in his hand.

I took it from him and read what was in it. The message said that No. 16 Woodville Crescent had been broken into while the occupants were out. Mr. Edmond Lorrimer, the owner, had returned with his wife to find the place ransacked. Articles of jewellery missing, together with £110 in money.

The address was not more than eight minutes' walk from The Drive on the city side!

'The motorist Big Joe stopped,' I said, 'he could be the fella who did this.' I handed the slip to Alderson and went on: 'Is the registration number known?'

'Joe got it, yes.' Alderson told me the number and added: 'It was a Mark 11 Jaguar, dove grey.'

'I take it all patrols have been alerted to look out for it?'

'Yes, that's been attended to.'

'Right. Let me know if they pick him up, will you?'

I was walking towards the doors when Alderson said: 'How're we going to let you know, P, if we can't find you?'

'I'll be back a bit later. Got some inquiries to make.

They turned out to be devoid of productive interest. I went back to Headquarters. Sergeant Alderson had an odd expression on his rugged face. 'We've checked the registration file—and there's no Jag or any other car, if it comes to that, with the number Big Joe reported,' he announced.

That could only mean one thing: the registration plate was a false one. Usually, crooks use stolen cars to make their getaway in. This one was presumably using his own, having substituted a fake number plate. And that in turn meant that he had looked up the file of registrations and invented a combination which did not clash with any other.

So the only clue we had was that he was driving a dove grey Jaguar. Well, there was no shortage of Jaguars and more than a few of that colour. And even if we rounded them all all up the one we were after would by now have reverted to its duly registered numbering.

'With this set-up, prospects don't look over-bright for catching the gang,' mused Alderson.

'We're not up against a gang this time,' I said. 'It's my belief that this—and very likely all the other recent unsolved crimes—is the work of a single operator with a proper job and living a highly respectable life.'

Alderson made a rueful grimace. 'That makes it look even more hopeless,' he commented.

'Well, while there's life there's hope,' I rejoined. 'And talking of life, I'm betting that this character is living the life of Riley . . .'

The sergeant leaned across the counter. 'Who *was* this fella Riley, anyway?' he asked interestedly.

'Blest if I know, but I've an idea that it's a clue.'

I went out again on the town. There were a number of spots where a man with a pocketful of loot might conceivably be living it up and I began a systematic comb-out.

It was in the Wagon Wheel Club that I got the first hint of a lead. Frankie Neilson, who was making a packet out of the bookying business, was drinking a large brandy at the bar.

'Hello, Mr. Prendergast,' he said. 'Didn't know you were a member.'

'I'm a member of more clubs than you might guess,' I said. 'There's an advantage in being able to walk in as of right.'

Frankie, a lean fellow with a deep cleft down each cheek, eyed me shrewdly. 'So you're after something, are you . . . or someone?'

'Just information.'

'What sort of information?'

I bought myself a small Scotch and said: 'Know any fella who's been having unusually large bets lately?'

He laughed. 'I've got several clients who do business with me regularly and in fairish sums. Nothing wrong about that, is there?'

'Depends.'

'You mean it depends whose money they're wagering, I suppose.' He drank some of his drink and added: 'The fellas I'm talking about are prosperous businessmen. I'll not tell you who they are, but you can take it from me they're all right. Why, what's on your mind?'

'I'm trying to solve a run of break-ins. Posh homes up on The Drive, all round that area. I've a theory they've been done by a talented amateur who may well be splashing the money around.'

'I get it. Well, I'll give a thousand to one he's not among *my* clients. Sorry I can't help.'

'It was just a chance,' I said.

'Sure and I'd have helped if I could . . .' Neilson broke

off to call a greeting across my shoulder: 'Hallo, Ricky. How's tricks?'

'Fine. How're they with you?'

'The same. By the way, meet an old pal of mine—Bill Prendergast, Ricky Mallory.'

I was saying how-do-you-do when Neilson added: 'Bill here is a C.I.D. 'tec, so mind your p's and q's!' He grinned broadly as he spoke. Ricky Mallory's face was oddly without expression. He was a young fellow, not more than twenty-six or -seven, expensively but unobtrusively dressed, and his voice carried the inflexions you can acquire only at the better type of public school.

'A pleasure to meet you, Mr. Prendergast,' he said. 'Would you care for another drink?'

'No, I don't think so. By the way, you wouldn't by any chance be the son of J. B. Mallory, would you?'

Young Mallory, who was in the act of squirting soda water into his Scotch, paused and said: 'As a matter of fact, yes. Why, do you know my father?'

'I met him once in the course of some inquiries,' I answered. The resemblance was noticeable without being over-strong. It was possible to see J. B. Mallory as he might have been at his son's age, though in other ways it was less possible. There was a nervous restlessness about Ricky Mallory which, I thought, would be alien to J.B. at any period in his life. Nor did he possess the schooled lack of expression which his son affected—and I felt certain it was an affectation. I wondered why. The public school manner, perhaps? The father left elementary school at fourteen, went straight to a firm of shipping agents and later had various jobs connected with shipping, studying three nights a week at technical classes. By the time he was twenty he was in business on his own account. Thirty-five years later, which meant the time of this story, he was a rich and reputedly hard man. He probably was. Few men succeed in amassing great wealth without the streak of cold steel in their natures; a measure of ruthlessness, too.

'Quite a character in our town, your dad,' I said. 'Rugged, eh? One of the old school.'

'*Yes*,' said Ricky Mallory, and rarely had I heard a monosyllable uttered in a tone of such bitter venom. Almost instantly he resumed in a relaxed drawl: 'Yes, Father is one of the few genuine characters left these days.' But it was too late. I had heard a single word which betrayed the accumulated, indwelling resentment, perhaps even hate, of a son for his father.

'Well, it's been a pleasure meeting you,' I said, 'but I'll have to be on my way. Give my respects to your dad, eh?'

'I'll do that, Mr. Prendergast,' he said carelessly.

I went out of the club. There was a parking area down the side. Eleven cars were on it, but no dove grey Jaguar. An all-white Austin Healey 3000 could be the one young Mallory had arrived in. I wrote the number down and when we checked it later it was his all right.

I went back to Headquarters and had a message radioed to the Z-car squads. This was a general message to keep looking for the Jaguar. We put a special one out to Z Victor One, taking the car off route to watch for an all-white Austin Healey 3000 driven by Richard Granville Mallory—and tail it.

'For Pete's sake, you don't think J.B.'s boy has something to do with the break-ins,' said Goodyard.

'I think it's a possibility,' I rejoined.

'If you're right his old man'll have forty-five fits,' said Sam.

'Then for his sake I hope I'm wrong.'

'But you don't believe you are?'

'No, but I could be, just the same. Resentment against

his father doesn't automatically make the son a housebreaker. What interests me is whether young Mallory runs the Austin Healey I saw on the parking space.'

'You're not the only one. Old Mallory is a tight-wad. He'd need to be in his dotage to put up the money for a car like that—and he isn't.'

The door opened and a constable on clerical duty came in. He reported that the vehicle was registered in the name of Richard Granville Mallory.

Sam looked across at me. 'It's still not conclusive, you know,' he said. 'The boy could have inherited money or something. In any case, old Mallory must know if his boy owns such a car.'

'Unless he keeps it somewhere else,' I replied.

'That's possible. But what about the Jaguar? We haven't had a report of one being stolen.'

'I agree that's puzzling. It can't be his father's either. Old Mallory runs a Bentley and has done for the last ten years—the same one, I mean.'

'I wonder . . .' Sam stopped and glanced at the door. Alderson had thrust his grizzled head round it.

'Z Victor One reports having lost contact with the Austin Healey,' he announced laconically.

'Damn!' said the D.I. 'What the hell are they playing at?'

'Apparently a lorry came out of a side road in front of them and they had to stop to avoid a collision. The car got too far in front to follow.' Alderson smiled faintly. 'I gather they had something to say to the lorry driver.'

'Bloody cowboy,' said Goodyard bitterly. 'Where did this happen?'

'That road up from the docks leading to the East Lancs.'

'Then young Mallory wasn't driving home,' I said. 'It's nowhere near there. Where's Z Victor One now?'

'They're coming in for fresh instructions, thought they'd better see you personally.' Alderson cocked his head to one side. 'That'll be them now.'

I went out into the main office. Jock and Bert were looking a trifle crestfallen.

'Sorry about what happened, but . . .' began Bert.

'Not your fault,' I said. 'Come on, let's go.'

'Where? Don't we have to get back on the normal route?'

'Not just yet. You can drive me out where you followed the Healey. I want to take a look round.'

We went through the city centre, finally making a right-hand turn and on to the long thoroughfare which connects with the East Lancashire Road. Bert Rawlings, who was driving, brought the Z-car to a halt at the spot where the lorry had rumbled out.

'We certainly told that fella a thing or two for the good of his health,' he said with a grin.

'I dare say. Did the sports car keep straight on from here?'

'As far as we could judge, yes.'

'Did you use your radio to contact Information and the other Z-cars?'

Jock nodded. 'Aye, we asked them to look out for a white Austin Healey and gave the registration number.'

'And nobody's spotted it?'

'Can't have, P. Why, what's running through your mind?'

'I have an idea that car's kept somewhere in the district we're now in, Jock. There must be a dozen places round here a fella could rent, if he wanted.'

Bert looked dubious. 'Like trying to find a ruddy needle in a haystack,' he said.

'Drive on slowly,' I directed.

'Right.' Bert let his clutch in and we drifted down

the long road. We went past dispirited pubs, fish-and-chip shops, factories and assorted warehouses. Some of them had an abandoned look. Still, who would hire a warehouse just to keep a car out of sight? Bert drove on, still in third gear. Now there were widening gaps between the buildings, and after a little while desolate tracts of land littered with the rubble left by demolition gangs.

A short way ahead a road went down to the left. I could see a rickety building, not much more than a shack. A light came from it, then abruptly went off.

'Stop!' I rapped. 'And switch your lights off for a minute.'

Bert cruised the car into the side and then mounted the pavement. We didn't even have to wait a minute. A car nosed out of the building. Someone got out and closed the doors and climbed back into the car. It was an all-white Austin Healey.

The driver halted at the mouth of the side road, then started to turn left. In the same instant Bert flicked all our lights on, including the blue winker on the roof. The main beam hit the white sports car full on its side. The driver turned a startled face. He was Ricky Mallory.

He didn't stop. There was a deep waffle from his exhaust as he gunned the big engine and streaked down the roadway. Bert didn't speak. He went fast through the gears. We were doing seventy in third before he changed up into top.

'Radio Information to alert all Z-cars and neighbouring forces,' I said.

Jock got through, raising the pitch of his voice over the mounting surge of the engine. The Austin Healey was far in the distance.

'Fella must be touching ninety,' said Bert. His foot slammed harder down on the accelerator pedal. We were out on the East Lancashire Road now, streaking down the dual carriageway in the second lane. So was Ricky Mallory. A car loomed ahead of him. He changed lanes, cutting in front of another car with what looked like inches to spare.

'God Almighty, the crazy bastard'll kill himself—or somebody else,' yelled Jock.

The car in the nearside lane had come almost to a stop. We could see the driver's white and trembling facc as we went past. Then we were on a long straight section emptied of traffic. It was a chance to gain on the white car—but it was similarly a chance for Ricky Mallory and he was using it.

Nobody spoke. I sat there watching the speedometer needle climbing into the nineties. There was no sign of the quarry. He was out-distancing us. Then, suddenly, we saw him—no more than a blur far ahead.

'He'll have to slow down,' said Bert. 'It's the access point to the M6.'

'Get as close as possible,' I said. 'I want to see if he turns on to the motorway.'

We reached the big sweep in the road. There was no sign of the Austin Healey. 'Get on to the M6,' I ordered. 'He'll reckon that's his best chance of losing us.'

We went down the slip road and out on to the motorway. There was no traffic behind us. Bert crossed to the fast lane. We were doing nearly a hundred miles an hour with all the lights blazing.

Minutes passed. Then Jock said impassively: 'Austin Healey now in view, Sarge.'

It was a white blob in the headlights. And we were gaining on it. Yet it was a faster car, both in maximum speed and tremendous power of acceleration. Bert sat without movement, his hands rock-steady on the wheel—the distance narrowing.

Then, suddenly, the Healey slowed, lunged leftwards

right across the three lanes and came to a crash stop. Ricky Mallory jumped out and sped to the side. We were on the Thelwall Viaduct which crosses the Manchester Ship Canal.

Bert had already cut his speed, glancing in the driving mirrors and then, swiftly, over his shoulder. No traffic. He crossed the broad sweep of the motorway, running in behind the Healey.

'He's climbing on the bloody parapet!' yelled Jock.

But I was already out of the Z-car and racing towards the spot. Ricky Mallory was clambering on it, struggling to stand upright when I reached him. I shot out both hands, grabbing at his ankles.

He made a single high scream, like a thin tormented nerve quivering in the night air. Then he toppled over backwards. I caught him as he fell.

'You're too young for that, son,' I said. 'You've got all your life in front of you.'

'I . . . I thought I could swim for it,' he said.

'At this point you'd have hit the ground,' I told him.

He stood up. 'So you've saved my life, eh?' he said. A bitter expression visited his handsome face. 'A pity because it's hardly worth saving. I suppose you're on to mc . . . I mean you know about the robberies and all that?'

'Suspicion is the word.'

He shrugged. 'Well, you'll have all the evidence you require, Mr. Prendergast,' he said. 'It's in the car. The stuff I got tonight, I mean. I was worried when you spoke to me in that club. So I put it in the Healey and was going to hide it somewhere—or even dump it. I'm afraid I was . . . well, scared.'

'Yes,' I answered. 'Like you were driving the Healey. You ought to have lost us but you hadn't the nerve to let it out to the full, had you?'

'No.'

'What about the Jag you used—whose is it?'

'It belongs to an aunt, she lets me borrow it. I just switch the number plates.'

'And you bought the Healey with some of the proceeds of your break-ins and keep it out of your father's sight and knowledge, eh?'

'Yes.' He looked at me for a long moment, then said: I'm twenty-three. He treats me like a schoolboy—worse. Do you know what he pays me for working in his damned office? Five pounds fifteen a week and my keep and clothes.'

'He belongs to the old school,' I said. 'He came up the hard way and he probably thinks that's how you ought to do it.'

'For God's sake, we're not living in the early 1920s . . .'

'Try and see it his way, son. After all, you'll inherit the business one of these days.'

'I hate him!'

'I'm sorry if you do, though I doubt it. And turning housebreaker isn't going to help you, is it?'

He bit down on his lip. 'No, I suppose not,' he admitted.

'Are you fit to drive?' I asked.

He nodded dumbly and I said: 'I'll sit with you.'

We were back on the East Lancashire Road and approaching the fringe of the city when he said: 'This is going to break Father, isn't it?'

'It'll hurt him, yes, but I think you may get a surprise.'

'I don't understand.'

'You dad is a tough man in business, he's had to be. But I happen to know several people who've been quietly helped by him. Kindnesses he's never wished to be made public. There's another side to your old man. Happen he's never shown it to you?'

'If he has I missed it,' said Ricky Mallory.

'Perhaps you've just not come up to his expectations. Perhaps, subconsciously, you've resented his success. He'd sense that, you know, and it's probably made him a little bitter, too.'

Young Mallory drove on. We were nearly at Police Headquarters before he spoke again. Then he said slowly: 'I never looked at it that way. Dad gave me a far better education than he had. I suppose he believed would equip me to take over when the time came. But . . . well, we seem to be perpetually at odds when I came down from the university. It was like trying to bridge an unbridgeable gap. I suppose it began when I was at public school. I never wanted to go to one, you know, and I had a bad time there at first. That was when I began to feel bitter about him.'

I got out of the car and we walked across the police parking yard. 'I have an idea your old man will stand by you,' I said.

Ricky Mallory got his chance—both from the magistrates and his father. The court was able to deal with him as a first offender and he was placed on probation for two years. Old Mallory said little, but what he did say was more than enough.

'I realised my son resented me, Mr. Prendergast,' he reflected. 'What he didn't know was that I resented him . . . the underlying envy of the old for the young. Perhaps we've both been damned fools. Well, things are going to be different, I can tell it.' He eyed me directly and added: 'You've been talking to him, I gather.'

'We did have a bit of a chat, sir.'

'Ricky has a big future with the company,' he rejoined. 'Perhaps even better than that, he and I suddenly seem to have a future together. I have the feeling that something you've said has made him see the light.'

'I'm glad,' I said.

All this happened years ago. Old J. B. Mallory is retired now and the boy who turned crook just for resentment and kicks is in charge. Once a year we meet for a drink. It is always the anniversary of the night we had that bit of a chat.

Big Joe Standy no longer does traffic control. He instructs young recruits instead. He always tells them: 'When ya pull a car up ya never want to go round the driver's side . . . it's better from t'other side, ya see.'

But he never tells them why he gives this advice.

10

The Human Factor

I was returning to Headquarters in Z Victor One when the radio message came through: *Smash-and-grab raid at jeweller's shop in Hester Street owned by T. Marcus and Son . . . proceed there immediately . . .*

Bert Rawlings made a right-hand turn at the next traffic signals, taking the shortest route.

'That makes three cases of smash-and-grab in the past month—since Terry Langham came out of Walton,' he reflected.

'You may be putting two and two together and making six,' I said. 'We'll need something more substantial than coincidence, Bert.'

'It's the sort of job Terry does as well as any of the villains and better'n most, you know that,' replied Bert doggedly.

'I'm not denying it, but so far there's been nothing to suggest it's young Terry. We checked his movements at the time of the previous cases and he had a good enough alibi.'

'It's him for sure, just the same, P.'

'Well,' I said, 'let's see what we can find out this time.'

What we found added up to precisely nothing in terms of evidence. A brick wrapped in cloth had smashed the window in, then three protecting steel bars had been forced apart with a lever sufficiently to allow the raider to grab some rings and watches. The haul was relatively small, but he had had to work fast in case he was seen and it would have taken a lot of time to lever the remaining bars. In the event, he had got away with articles valued at £357. Even when fenced at a considerably lower figure it was top pay for a few minutes' work . . . if you didn't get caught.

The wrapped brick was still there and so was the crowbar he had used as a lever, but neither carried any fingerprints—and there were no other clues and nobody had seen him.

A courting couple passing along the little street had spotted the smashed window and the young fellow had dialled 999.

'The street was empty when we turned into it,' he said.

'You didn't catch a glimpse of anyone running down it?' I asked.

He shook his head. 'Not a sign—we didn't see a thing, did we Glad?'

The blonde girl who was with him said no, they didn't see a thing. 'It was just like Bill says, sir—the street was deserted. Then Bill saw the broken window and dashed into a phone box to tell you fellas.'

Old Mr. Marcus's son, who had been summoned from his home, gave us a list of the stolen articles and we drove back towards Headquarters. We were half-way along Lime Street when I said suddenly: 'Stop the car, Bert.'

He signalled to following traffic and brought the Z-car to a standstill. A slim young chap had just stepped out of a pub and was walking towards us.

I wound the rear window down, poked my head out and said: 'Hello, Terry!'

Terry Langham slackened his stride. He had both

hands in his trousers pockets and was making a little breathy kind of whistling sound between his lips. When he saw me he quit whistling and grinned.

'Why, if it's not Mr. P and a couple of t'lads,' he said. 'Nice to see you and what can I be doing for you?'

'D'you know Hester Street, by any chance?'

He speared fingers through his thick dark hair. 'Sure and I know it well,' he replied. 'Why?'

'You wouldn't happen to have been there this evening, would you?'

He chuckled. 'If I want a bit of life I don't go down there and that's a fact,' he said.

'All right, where *have* you been?'

The amiability ebbed from his smooth face. 'What's it to you?' he demanded. 'Just because you fellas have put me down a time or two doesn't mean you got a right to pester me.'

'You haven't answered the question, Terry,' I said curtly. 'I'm still asking—where *were* you all evening?'

'Lemme see,' he considered. 'Oh, yes, I had me tea. Then I had a shave and a bit of a wash and changed me clothes. That's right. Then I thought I'd nip out for a few jars and see me pals . . . that's how you come to see me leaving thc boozer . . .' He jerked his head in its direction.

'And you haven't been in Hester Street?'

He leaned in at the open window. 'If you want to know the truth, I don't think I've ever been there in me life,' he said. 'I know where it is, that's all.'

'I see. Well, just the same, you'll not object to helping the police in some inquiries, will you?'

'I got something better to do than sit around answering a lot of questions that don't concern me,' he said.

'So you decline to assist us, eh?'

His face, which had gone tight, relaxed. The amiable grin was back in position. 'I didn't say that, Mr. P,' he murmured. 'Naturally, I'll help you lads.' Without any more ado, he opened the door. I moved back along the seat and he slid in. 'Never let it be said Terry Langham wouldn't help the ruddy Jacks to the very best of his knowledge and belief,' he said.

'Thanks,' I replied drily.

'Think nothing of it, Mr. P. . . . I'm dee-lighted to oblige,' grinned Terry.

I knew then that we weren't going to find anything incriminating on him. Nor did we. I tried the wearing-down technique of the interrogation—the patient, remorseless, respective questioning under which a man will often contradict himself, forget a previously-related lie or betray some small meaningful detail.

But Terry Langham just sat there in the interviewing room blandly sticking to the essentials of his story. He hadn't been anywhere near Hester Street, had never heard of Marcus and Son, had spent the evening boozing.

'Not heavily, you understand, Mr. P—but a pint or two of the old black-and-tan.' He chuckled again. 'Well, happen more than a pint or two. Four jars of wallop it was, but not enough to make me say daft things to the Jacks.'

'You mean you're keeping something back?'

He waved an airy hand. 'Not a sausage. I've told you the truth. Hey—why don't you ask in that pub you saw me come out of? Somebody must have seen me.'

'I thought you were out with your mates.'

He shrugged. 'They never turned up, the so-and-so's. I had a nice little session all on me ownsome, like. Kept waiting, first in one pub then in another, but they never came.'

'Well,' I said, 'since you are as white and innocent as

the driven snow, you won't mind us taking you home and having a look round, will you?'

'Not at all, suit your ruddy selves,' answered Terry Langham. 'But I've changed me lodge.'

'Oh, where are you now then?'

'I'm lodging with Molly Grierson.' He said it casually, but for the first time there was a wary look in his blue eyes.

I made no comment, but another train of thought was starting to run through my mind. Molly Grierson was a strong, boldly handsome woman about forty. She was a prostitute.

We put Terry Langham back in the Z-car and were approaching the address he had given, which was near Mount Pleasant, when I said: 'Molly Grierson's on the game.'

'Well?'

'I just wondered if you knew.'

'If I did it's got nowt to do with me, has it? If you're trying to put the arm on me for living on her you can damned well think again.'

'I didn't suggest that, Terry,' I said. 'Anyway, she's a bit old for you—about a dozen years older, I'd say.'

'It's a comfortable lodge and Molly looks after me fine and that's all there is to it,' he said.

Molly opened the door to us. She wasn't entertaining any gentlemen friends. The house was old and shabby but everything in it was neat and clean.

'Hell's bells!' she exclaimed. 'A visit from the Jacks. Well, that wants chalking up and no mistake.' Her clear gaze shifted from Terry to me. 'What's my young lodger supposed to have done then?' she demanded.

'He's just giving us a bit of help in some inquiries we're making,' I answered. 'Jock—you go on up with Terry to his room.'

'I'll show you the way, *Mister* Ewing,' said Terry sardonically.

When they had gone up the stairs, Molly Grierson said evenly: 'I hope you're not pestering Terry just on account of he's been inside.'

'We have no intention of hounding him, if that's what you mean.'

'Oh, well then, I'm glad. He's a good lodger, pays regular and never causes me any bother.'

I looked at her for a moment. 'I didn't know you took in a lodger,' I ventured.

'Why shouldn't I?'

'No reason, except that I'd have thought a lodger on the premises might be inconvenient, Molly.'

'You mean because I'm on the game,' she answered coolly.

'Yes.'

'Well, it's all right. Terry has his own room and, anyway, he goes out most nights.' She gave me a mocking look. 'Happen you'd like to call round some night.'

'And happen I wouldn't. How did you meet him?'

'In a pub . . .' She stopped.

I said: 'You mean a pick-up?'

'No, it wasn't like that. He was asking the barman about finding digs and I thought he looked a nice young fella and on the spur of the moment I said he could lodge here.'

'I see. You never had a lodger before, did you?'

'No.' She reached for a packet of cigarettes. The movement brought her closer. I could smell gin.

I had a sudden thought and said: 'I suppose you've been in all night?'

She snicked a match into flame, dragged on the cigarette and said carelessly: 'That's right, I didn't want to go out this evening. I had some things to see to. Why?'

'Nothing.'

Jock came back into the room with Terry. A few moments later we were in the car. 'Nothing in his room, P,' announced Jock.

The driver said: 'Looks like Terry's not our man, then.'

'Things don't always look the way they are,' I answered enigmatically.

'What's that mean?'

'Molly Grierson smelled of gin and tonic, but she told me she'd been in all evening.'

'Heck, she might have a bottle in the house.'

'I didn't see any, Jock. If she'd been drinking the bottle would most likely be out.'

'What are you getting at, then?'

'I'm just wondering if she *did* go out, that's all.'

'Well, suppose she did—what about it?'

'She could have met Terry Langham after the smash-and-grab but before we spotted him coming out of that pub.'

Bert whistled. 'You mean he could have passed the stuff to her, is that it?'

'I'm considering it as a tenable theory,' I replied.

II

A fortnight later it still looked like a tenable theory, but I still hadn't found anything which would even begin to substantiate it.

Then, one afternoon, while I was crossing Lime Street opposite St. George's Hall, someone spoke my name—and, turning, I saw Molly Grierson. There was usually something slightly flamboyant about her appearance, but now she was more quietly attired. The clothes she had on looked new and they hadn't been bought in any bargain basement.

'How's Terry Langham?' I asked.

'Oh, he's fine,' she replied. 'He's working as a storekeeper, somewhere in the docks.'

'You're looking very smart today,' I said.

She glanced down at herself. 'So you like the outfit, eh? Bit on the quiet side for me.' She laughed and added: 'It's sort of apt, like. I've given up the game, you see.'

I didn't say anything and she went on: 'My daughter's coming home to live with me, so I reckoned it was time to quit.'

'I didn't know you ever had a daughter, Molly.'

'Ah, well, you don't know everything about me. And you wouldn't know about my having Christine, anyway. She's been at a convent school and then she went to live with her auntie in the Midlands. But now she's coming home. She's just twenty-one and I certainly don't want her to know her mam was a whore.'

'Well, I'm glad,' I said. 'But what are you going to do about money?'

'Oh, that? I'm not short, you know. I looked after the lolly all right.'

'That's more than most of the girls in your late profession do then.'

'Don't I know it! Well, I didn't toss the stuff around. I've got quite a nest-egg, then there's Terry's lodging money and Christine will have a job. I'll manage quite nicely, thank you.'

'That's fine and I hope everything works out for you.'

'It will—you can bank on it,' said Molly Grierson.

We parted and I walked on slowly, my mind filled with thought. Prostitutes are big spenders. Like the tearaways, with them it's easy come easy go and there's plenty more where that came from. It was true that there are some who look after their money and, of course, it's tax-free. But I knew Molly Grierson as a woman who liked feminine finery and, even more to the point, drinking in company. It was difficult to credit that she had 'quite a nest-egg'—at least, if by that she meant plenty of money to live on without returning to her immoral mode of life.

Also, I still had the feeling that Terry Langham was the man behind the recent robberies. If I was right about this, it was not inconceivable that Molly was hiding the loot . . . or fencing it. Perhaps that was why she could afford to quit going on the game.

I resolved to keep my eyes very wide open and to make a number of undercover inquiries. I explained what I had in mind to Sam Goodyard and went out that same night. A detective comes to have various sources of information—some of them specific, others adding up to no more than indirect suggestions or guarded hints—but my initial inquiries along these lines seemed to be singularly barren.

Then a small, unexpected incident occurred. I was approaching a café along the Dock Road when two figures emerged, going away from me. But I had recognised both of them. One was Molly Grierson, the other was Fred Harman, and he was one of us—an elderly Jack not far off retirement. Fred Harman belonged to the old school—hard, cynical, scoffing at changing methods and technical advances in police work, but routinely efficient and immensely knowledgeable; his close-cropped bony head was packed with thirty-odd years of not exactly elevating experience. And he was walking into the dimness of the Dock Road with Molly Grierson.

I stood quite still, watching them disappear. I didn't think Detective-Constable Harman was going with her in order to have her. It was possible, of course, but I simply did not believe it. Fred Harman used people for one purpose only—to get information. Also, Molly had obviously spoken with complete sincerity about quitting—a sincerity reinforced by the fact that the last thing she wanted was for her young daughter to know her past life.

That left me with one alternative: Molly Grierson was playing the informer. But about what and about whom?

I didn't have long to wait before I knew. Forty-eight hours later Fred Harman came through the main entrance at Police Headquarters with Terry Langham handcuffed to him.

'Attempted smash-and-grab at Hennecker's store in Fallon Street,' Harman said. 'That's the charge I'm making, and it'll stick all right—I caught this fella right in the bloody act.'

Terry eyed him balefully: 'You didn't have to march me through t'streets in handcuffs, you lousy Jack,' he said tightly. 'I'd have come quiet like.'

'He would have done, Fred,' I remarked. 'This fella isn't one of the violent kind.'

'When I want advice from you, P, I'll ask for it,' said Harman. He grinned wolfishly. 'Besides, it takes the shine outa these villains to be seen with the bracelets on 'em. I like that.'

'Yeh, you would,' said Terry bitterly. 'Who grassed on me?'

'I just happened to be on the spot,' Harman said. 'Not that it was sheer blind luck—I been keeping tabs on you for a bit, see?'

'Funny I never saw you even once then,' replied Terry Langham slowly. 'You want to know what I think?'

'I don't give a damn what you think, fella. All I care about is that I'm putting you down.'

'I think you're a bloody liar, that's what,' said Terry calmly.

Harman made a hard ball with his right fist, but almost immediately he uncoiled his fingers and shrugged. 'It doesn't matter what you think,' he sneered. 'It's what the Stipe thinks when you stand in the dock. Or, better still, the judge.'

A uniformed man took Terry Langham down to the cells. I was sitting in the C.I.D. room turning a few things over in my mind when Fred Harman strolled in.

'The judge'll give him three years,' he said.

'I doubt it.'

'Oh, why?'

'He's young and doesn't have much of a record and doesn't commit violence,' I answered. 'It's my guess the Stipendiary will deal with this case.'

Harman shrugged and went out. I could see by the look of his back what he thought. But I was right, all the same. Terry Langham got nine months.

Molly Grierson wasn't in court. But a dark-haired young girl suddenly burst into sobs and rushed towards the dock.

'Terry . . . Terry,' she wailed. 'I can't bear the thought of you going away . . .'

A uniformed constable touched her arm. 'Don't take on, miss,' he said kindly, 'you'll be able to see him before they take him to prison.'

He took her down below. I waited for her. When she came back I said: 'Are you Miss Christine Grierson?'

'Yes—who are you?'

'Prendergast, C.I.D.'

'Oh . . .' She hesitated and then went on: 'Not the detective who arrested my Terry?'

'No, that was Detective Constable Harman. What did you mean about calling him your Terry?'

'We love each other,' she said simply.

'You realise he's committed an offence, and that this isn't the first time?'

'I don't care what he's done,' she cried passionately. 'I love him . . . didn't you hear what I said?'

'Yes, I heard, Miss Grierson.' I walked with her on to the steps leading from the court down to the street. 'What does your mother think?'

For a moment she didn't answer. Her beautiful mouth went hard in a long, compressed line. When she looked directly at me her eyes had an odd sort of flicker.

'I haven't asked her,' she said, and ran on down the steps.

III

Months passed. There were no more crimes which looked like the handiwork of young Terry Langham. But there were others, more than enough to keep the C.I.D. strength and the Z-car squads busy.

Then, on a warm night in mid-September, Terry Langham came to see me. He was paler than when I last saw him, but he looked fit enough.

'I've been out of jail several days,' he mentioned.

'So I believe. Where are you living—the same place?'

'Yes, I went back there.' He made a hard laugh. 'The one place I'm never going back to is prison,' he added.

'Well, there are better places, I agree.'

'I'm never going back, Mr. P—that's what I've come to tell you, so's you'll not get ideas about me.'

'You mean such as looking for you in connection with the next crime that's reported to us?'

'That's right. I'm going to marry Christine and we plan to emigrate to Australia. So you don't need to give me a thought.'

'I wish you luck,' I said. 'What about Molly Grierson?'

'I don't know what you're talking about,' he said quickly. Too quickly.

'You just gave yourself away, Terry. The question could have been no more than an ordinary inquiry about how a mother feels at the prospect of her daughter going a long way away. But you reacted differently.'

'Shut up,' he whispered. 'I don't want to think about that.'

'About the fact that you were living with Molly, really living with her? That's how it was between you, wasn't it?'

He nodded, not speaking.

I went on: 'Then Christine came home and you fell in love. All that makes sense, though not perhaps to Molly.'

Suddenly, his jaw squared. 'I'll kill her if she tries to come between us,' he said.

'That wouldn't help you and Christine, would it—you getting life?'

'No, but she better not interfere . . .'

I thought Molly Grierson had probably been both mistress and mother to him, and that's a dangerous combination. I also thought two other things, but I mentioned only one of them.

'Did Molly fence the loot for you?' I asked.

A faint grin flickered on his face. Then, as suddenly, it was gone and he said: 'I might answer that if you told me who tipped off Fred Harman the night he booked me.'

'I don't know,' I said.

But I had already guessed . . . months ago.

Three nights later Terry Langham was in the cells again. Fred Harman had made the arrest—and once again he 'chanced' to be on the scene at the precise moment.

When Terry was locked up I said: 'Where did you get your information, Fred?'

'No information, I was just keeping my eye on that young tearaway, that's all.'

'I wasn't born yesterday, even though I'm younger than you,' I said.

'What's that supposed to mean?'

'I'll answer that with another question, Fred: how well do you know Molly Grierson?'

The coarse skin on his face flushed dully. 'I've never so much as spoken to her,' he snapped and went straight out.

For a man with a lot of not always elevating experience he was a bad liar.

Terry Langham was put up in court next day and remanded in custody for a week. Several nights later I was off duty, looking forward pleasurably to my favourite recreation—reading. I had got no more than half-way through a chapter when the phone rang.

My wife Alice took the call and said: 'It's for you, Bill—a young man he sounds, name of Langham.'

'You must be joking,' I replied. 'Terry Langham's in custody.'

'He isn't, you know—he's on the phone,' said my wife calmly. Few things, especially those having to do with police work, surprise her.

I got up and spoke down the receiver. The answering voice belonged to Terry Langham, there was no question about that.

'I've escaped,' he said. 'Before they get me back there's two things I wanted to tell you, so I got on the blower.'

'I'm listening,' I answered.

'I found something out, something I've really known all the time but couldn't bring myself to believe.' There was a small pause, then he said on a rising note: 'Are you still there?'

'Yes.'

'I found out it was Molly who grassed on me, both times—on account of she was mad jealous over me and Christine. Right from the start, from the minute Christine came home. I suppose she could tell we'd fallen for each other. Well, she informed on me to that lousy Jack, Fred Harman. I found out she's been tipping him off about other things . . .'

'Go on,' I said.

'You want to know what the second thing is,' he said harshly.

In fact, I already had a premonition of what he was going to say.

'I told you I'd kill Molly if she came between me and Christine . . . well, she's done it, see?' His voice ascended a scale of near-hysteria. 'D'you understand what I mean, Mr. P?'

'Yes, I understand,' I said. I clapped a hand over the mouthpiece and called to my wife.

'I'm going to do her in,' said Terry Langham in a tight, ice-cold voice. She'll not squeal on me again.' He laughed stridently and went on: 'I'm using the call-box only a minute from the house . . . a little more'n sixty seconds she's got . . .'

'Use the next-door phone, Alice. Call information and tell them to alert the nearest Z-car to Molly Grierson's address . . . they know it . . .' I took my hand away and said: 'Look, Terry, will you listen?'

'You ain't got a thing to say that'll stop me now, Mr. P . . .'

'Don't do anything desperate Terry. You want to go on living and not inside a prison, don't you? Think of Christine . . . give yourself up and . . .'

'You're wasting your time, Mr. P,' he said. 'Good-bye!'

I slammed the receiver down. I could hear my breath coming harshly down my nose and my hands felt damp with perspiration. The door opened and Alice said: 'The phone next door . . . it's out of order . . .'

I used ours, speaking fast. The alert would go out within seconds. Perhaps too much time hadn't been lost—but he had said he was in a kiosk only a minute away from Molly Grierson's house. I raced out and got my own car. More seconds, seeming endless.

All sets of traffic signals were green as I got to them. Even so, I was breaking the speed limit all the way. Z Victor One was outside Molly Grierson's house when I arrived. I ran inside. Jock Ewing was on one knee close to Molly Grierson. The back of her head looked as if it had caved in. The room was in disorder and spattered with blood. Nobody ever looked more dead.

IV

Terry Langham just strolled into Police Headquarters. He looked pale but composed. There was some blood on his hands and etching the side of his white collar. The cars were still out hunting for him.

'I've come to give myself up,' he said. 'I told you I'd do her and I did. You fellas couldn't get there in time to stop me—that's why I phoned your house. I worked out that it was your night off.'

'Show me your hands,' I said.

He held them both out, turning them slowly. There were cuts and bruises on them.

'Molly Grierson was badly knocked about,' I said.

'I hit her harder than I meant, Mr. P . . . she was in a flaming rage . . . screaming filthy insults at me . . . saying

I'd never have Christine, that she'd see me put away for twenty years first ... I suppose I went berserk.' He shrugged.

'Don't ask me to say I'm sorry. She had it coming to her and more.'

'She got it,' I said heavily. 'She's dead.'

For a second he stood there staring. Then his eyes blinked rapidly and an odd expression came into them, almost as if he had suddenly remembered something.

'Then I *must* have hit her much harder than I thought,' he said calmly.

'With your fists?'

'That's right, with my fists ... oh, and something I picked up, a poker or something, I was in such a blind rage I can't rightly remember.'

'You're not remembering any of the details very well, are you?' I said.

'What's it matter? I did it. All right, I didn't mean to kill her, never mind what I said to you. But it looks like I must've done. Go on, then—book me.'

We booked him.

I went back to the house. I didn't find a bloodstained poker or any kind of poker. I didn't find anything that could have caused the damage to the base of Molly Grierson's head.

I was on the point of leaving when Christine Grierson came in from the street. She looked at me and said:

'Why, what brings you here, Mr. Prendergast?'

'Your mam's been savagely attacked,' I told her.

'You ... you mean she's ...' Christine broke off. The unspoken word could have been 'dead', but I knew, without any means of proving it, that she had been going to say something very different, the exact opposite. She was leaning against the inside of the door, her face white and ravaged.

'She's been terribly assaulted,' I said.

The girl lurched sideways across the narrow hall, as if she were about to faint. I didn't even attempt to catch her because I knew she wasn't fainting. I knew it as surely as I also knew that I was never going to be able to prove the suspicion which was now a certainty.

'Can . . . can I see her?' she asked.

'She's not here.'

'Where is she then, in hospital?'

'Yes, in hospital.'

She turned to look directly at me; a long, almost unfathomable look.

'You're very curt, Mr. Prendergast,' she said levelly. 'Is Mother dead?'

'Yes. Terry Langham is in police custody, under arrest.'

She beat both her fists on my chest. 'He didn't do it, he didn't do it!' she shouted. 'He couldn't have done it . . . he escaped and was with me . . . that's where I've been . . . with Terry . . .'

'He's confessed, Christine,' I said.

This time I had to catch her as she went out in a dead faint.

We found the poker. It had been wiped clean of fingerprints, but you can't get rid of bloodstains quite so easily. Christine had thrown it onto a tip not far from her home.

'Mother found out we had married by special licence —it was just before Terry was remanded,' she said. 'We had a dreadful, horrible row . . . I didn't know such words could be used by any human being. I ran crying from the house. When I returned she was lying on the floor. Her face was bruised and cut, but when she saw me she started again and went for the poker . . . I got to it first . . . and, and . . .'

'You delivered the final blow,' I finished.

'Yes. I didn't mean to, I didn't know what I was doing. But it was me. You can't charge Terry now.'

'He's already confessed, Christine.'

'But you *can't* convict him!'

'He's admitted it—and a neighbour has come forward who saw him running from the house with blood on his hands shortly before we got there.'

'But I tell you *I* did it . . .'

I looked at her, not accusingly or harshly or in any special way. I was thinking, as I have too often had to do, of the wickedness and the frailty and the meaningless stupidity of human urges as they impinge on some people's lives. Terry Langham and Christine Grierson could have run away together, could have fled twelve thousand miles to the other side of the earth and Molly Grierson would never have followed. So she need never have died and two other lives need not have been scarred for ever. But the human factor makes nonsense of logic, just as it does with the grandiose plans of man.

'I know you did it, Christine, but Terry's taking the rap—the evidence is against him. Against you we have not even the start of a job. And you're his wife . . . leave it at that, Christine.'

I touched her slim hand. On a warm night it felt zero cold.

'Do you want to see Terry?'

'Please,' she said brokenly.

Terry Langham was sentenced to seven years for manslaughter after being found not guilty on the capital charge.

He earned full remission for good conduct. I knew the

date of his release and went to see him. He was pale, given to sudden deep silences and his hair was turning grey, though he was only thirty years old.

'I . . . waited for you, Terry,' faltered Christine. She had aged, too. Youth had gone from them, and with it all the gay *élan* of living.

I wondered if they would ever recapture its lovely, warm essence . . . but they went away to London and I never saw them again and never tried to find out.

11

The Summing-up

Ever since the long-vanished night when a broken old woman confided the strange tragedy of her life to a green young constable on his first assignment, I have sought to probe below the surface of human attitudes—to pull away the mask and see for myself what may lie underneath. It has helped me to understand why people behave the way they do; it has even caused me to find some gleams of human kindliness where you might justifiably suppose they did not exist.

But if this has made me more tolerant of human frailty, it must not be taken as implying that I belong to the currently fashionable avant-garde which often seems to be more concerned with the well-being of the criminal than with his victims.

That is why, in this summing-up of all the things I hold most strongly, I think first of the ordinary, decent hard-working citizens of this country whose lives have been irreparably wounded by the vicious and the ruthless. I think of the old man beaten into mental derangement by a tearaway's blackjack; I think of the life savings rifled from a helpless old lady; of the highly organised crimes of violence and plunder running into thousands and even millions of pounds; of young girls raped and murdered; of police officers who may go on duty even as you read this . . . and never return to their wives and children.

I have known tearaways with the spark of decency still burning within them, even if fitfully—and some of these I have helped, successfully, to a new and better life. But there are others, committed beyond the reformer's hand. I am thinking of the men who have made their decision sanely and coldly; the men who have deliberately placed themselves beyond the law. Now each one of us needs that secret sense of self-importance without which life itself is almost unendurable. We try to achieve this by the realisation of whatever talents and inherent qualities we may possess. But the avowed criminal does it by what is not less than a declaration of war against society.

What are we to do with such as these? I will tell you what one retired police detective thinks and feels in every fibre of his being. It is this: if any man decides to be an outlaw then we should make him one in fact—strip him of every civil right and privilege until the day when he abdicates from his illegal and self-chosen role.

As we moved towards the last three decades of this turbulent century I have to say, without qualification, that I regret the abolition of the capital sentence. I know and, to some degree, sympathise with the arguments of those who have secured its abandonment. It was John Donne who noted that any man's death diminishes us all. But it does not necessarily follow that we should flinch from the ultimate sanction by which society can defend itself—and, let us face it, exact just retribution.

The man who murders in cold blood has similarly and savagely ended the life of a fellow human being—sometimes a policeman, who for no lush rewards, is concerned solely in making our land safe for us all to go about in. For that and similar crimes the killer should face a penalty no less irrevocable.

It was recently suggested to me that in my next book I should print my view about corporal punishment. This I will now do. I do not want to see the barbarous cat-o'-nine tails brought back, but I believe that we have erred in eschewing the birch—particularly for the vicious breed of tearaways to whom casual violence and calculated sadism are required attributes. It is not an accident that this kind of thuggery is almost unknown in the Isle of Man, whose independent Parliament has insisted on retaining the right to use the birch.

It is the indignity of the procedure, as much as the physical pain, which throws blind panic into the craven bosoms of the bullies, the mindless tearaways who gloat over 'putting the boot in' when someone lies helpless at their feet—and, of course, is hopelessly outnumbered.

I am aware that the vociferous do-gooders—who I suspect, in no way represent the views of the majority of people—will rail at me, evoking the image of a brutalised copper without understanding or feeling for the psychological maladjustments of his unfortunate brethren. To all such well-intentioned persons I can only say that I hope they will never feel the crunch of the cosh, have their life savings stolen or their daughters forcibly despoiled.

I believe in the prevention as well as the detection of crime; I believe in the reformation as well as the punishment of criminals. All who can benefit from psychiatric help should have it. But, for God's sake, let us put first things first—and the first prerequisite for an ordered society is the protection of the good citizen. Just as no nation can repel aggression without strength and the certainty of its usage, so no society can defend itself from the predatory outlaws in its midst without the power to exact retribution.

I have known very, very few villains who ever came back for a second birching. But this is not all; I hold that the criminally maimed and the criminally dispossessed must be compensated *at the criminal's expense*—if need be for the whole period of the latter's life.

And, particularly at this time, any man who uses a car for crime and violence should face one absolute, inexorable and unalterable additional penalty: the total disqualification from driving for life.

I'd like to say something about juvenile delinquency—though I like the word juvenile little better than that other constantly used one, teenager. The fact is that teenagers are simply people who happen to be younger than some other people—not a newly discovered tribe of incomprehensible attitudes. Also, I think the majority are pretty good citizens. I have seen the dedication of young nurses and doctors. I know something of the work young people are doing in voluntary service—here and overseas. I see fine boys and girls going about their work and recreation in my own and other cities. One way and another, I think the nation is going to have some pretty good parents in the future. The difficult youngsters who get into the newspaper headlines are a minority. But it is undeniable that a stratum of delinquency exists and that, undeniably, it is not declining.

In a previous book I suggested that this is at least partly due to the diminishing influence of the father in the home, and I see no reason to amend that view. I now ask myself: is our probation system truly adequate?

I do not believe that it is; and in this connection I feel that not enough use is made of the working policeman's experience and knowledge in obtaining reports and assessing the background of young offenders. Instead of the probation officer appearing before the justices in juvenile cases we would do better to listen to the officer intimately concerned; be sure that he is much better equipped to know when the tale is being told, much more likely to possess an acute insight into the accused's background.

Finally, a word about the constitution of our police forces. To the Englishman the creation of a single national force is suspect—and rightly. The dangers of its misuse are apparent; it would take us, however unwittingly, a step along the road to the police state. New regional groupings, the fusion of very small forces—yes. But no more than that.

The expansion of the Z-cars idea—certainly. The new Panda patrols? Admirable—but not, I urge, as a replacement of the bobby on the beat. The Z-car squads can chase the modern desperado in his ultra-fast automobile—or, more accurately, the one he has just stolen from somebody else. The Pandas are a useful mobile patrol over more limited areas.

But there is not and never has been any substitute for the uniformed man patrolling the pavements of city and suburb, in town streets and along country lanes. How much safer we all feel when we nod good night to that helmeted figure as he passes by on a dark night—and how uneasy the wrongdoer feels!

So—let the punishment fit the crime, let the forces of law and order be modernised but not nationalised, let the mobile arms of the police be expanded and reinforced by every technological aid; but, no less, let us consolidate the pedestrian force on the beat.

For there are still far more pedestrians than motorists—and on this vital level the policeman should not only be known to exist but be seen!